AF405328

A Book Of

ORIGIN AND DEVELOPMENT OF GLOBAL BUSINESS

BBA (IB) (Semester - II) : Course Code 202

(CBCS Pattern 2019)

As Per New Syllabus, Effective from June 2019

Ameya Anil Patil
MBA (Finance), B.E. (Computer)
Assistant Professor,
(BBA, BBA-IB), SKNCC, STES,
Pune

Karan Rajeev Randive
M. Phil., M.Com., Ph.D. (Pursuing)
SNDT,
Pune

Prof. Ankita Bhatt
M. Phil., M.Com., SET, Ph.D. (Pursuing)
BBA, BBA (IB), B.Com.
SKNCC, STES,
Pune

Prof. Pradnya Bachhav
MBA (HR), BCA, Ph.D. (Pursuing)
BBA, BB (IB), SKNCC STES,
Pune

N4976

Origin and Development of Global Business (Sem. II)　　　**ISBN 978-93-89825-02-2**

First Edition　:　December 2019
©　　　　　:　Author

Published By:
NIRALI PRAKASHAN
Abhyudaya Pragati, 1312, Shivaji Nagar
Off J.M. Road, PUNE – 411005
Tel - (020) 25512336/37/39, Fax - (020) 25511379
Email : niralipune@pragationline.com

➤ **DISTRIBUTION CENTRES**

PUNE

Nirali Prakashan : 119, Budhwar Peth, Jogeshwari Mandir Lane, Pune 411002,
(For orders within Pune)　Maharashtra, Tel : (020) 2445 2044, Mobile : 9657703145
Email : niralilocal@pragationline.com

Nirali Prakashan : S. No. 28/27, Dhayari, Near Asian College Pune 411041
(For orders outside Pune)　Tel : (020) 24690204; Mobile : 9657703143
Email : bookorder@pragationline.com

MUMBAI

Nirali Prakashan : 385, S.V.P. Road, Rasdhara Co-op. Hsg. Society Ltd.,
Girgaum, Mumbai 400004, Maharashtra;
Mobile : 9320129587 Tel : (022) 2385 6339 / 2386 9976,
Fax : (022) 2386 9976
Email : niralimumbai@pragationline.com

➤ **DISTRIBUTION BRANCHES**

JALGAON

Nirali Prakashan : 34, V. V. Golani Market, Navi Peth, Jalgaon 425001,
Maharashtra, Tel : (0257) 222 0395, Mob : 94234 91860;
Email : niralijalgaon@pragationline.com

KOLHAPUR

Nirali Prakashan : New Mahadvar Road, Kedar Plaza, 1st Floor Opp. IDBI Bank,
Kolhapur 416 012, Maharashtra. Mob : 9850046155;
Email : niralikolhapur@pragationline.com

NAGPUR

Nirali Prakashan : Above Maratha Mandir, Shop No. 3, First Floor,
Rani Jhanshi Square, Sitabuldi, Nagpur 440012, Maharashtra
Tel : (0712) 254 7129;
Email : niralinagpur@pragationline.com

DELHI

Nirali Prakashan : 4593/15, Basement, Agarwal Lane, Ansari Road, Daryaganj
Near Times of India Building, New Delhi 110002
Mob : 08505972553, Email : niralidelhi@pragationline.com

BENGALURU

Nirali Prakashan : Maitri Ground Floor, Jaya Apartments, No. 99, 6th Cross,
6th Main, Malleswaram, Bengaluru 560003, Karnataka;
Mob : 9449043034
Email: niralibangalore@pragationline.com

Other Branches : Hyderabad, Chennai

niralipune@pragationline.com　|　www.pragationline.com
Also find us on 🄵 www.facebook.com/niralibooks

Preface ...

It gives us an immense pleasure to present this book on 'Origin and Development of Global Business', which covers the several aspects of a Globalized world. The subject introduces the students to the business carried across borders, that is, International Business. Industrialization, International trade theories, and International organizations of repute such as IMF, WTO, World Bank have been discussed in the book. A section has been devoted to understand the several options to gain an entry into International Business starting from Exports to Joint Ventures, Wholly owned subsidiaries, Acquisitions etc.

We are extremely grateful to Mr. Jignesh Furia for presenting us with this opportunity .

We would like to thank Mr. Amol Mahabal for putting together the myriad sections in this book and thereby, presenting this book in a systematic way.

We would also like to thank Mr. Ilyas Shaikh, and Mr. Prasad Chintakindi, Mrs. Anjali Muley for their valuable help in preparation of this book.

Finally, we express deep regards towards Sinhgad Technical Education Society for providing us an enabling and supportive environment for learning and teaching.

Suggestions for improvement of this book are always welcome.

AUTHOR

Origin and Development of Global Business : BBA IB (Sem-II)
Course Code 202

1. Industrial Development (Indian Context)

1. Introduction to Globalization, Concepts and Importance in Modern World Economy.
2. International Business and Domestic Business and Companies
3. Stages of Industralization, Means of Entry into the International Business

2. National and International Trade

1. Concept or National and International Trade in Modern World and its Contribution
2. Components of National and International Business
3. PESTEL Model (Social, Political, Technological, Economic Environment and Legal) of International Business
4. Geographical Indications - Nature, Concept and Importance.

3. Theories of International Trade

1. Difference between various Theories and its Merits and Limitations
2. Various Commercial Policy Tarrifs and Non-tariffs Measures – National and International

4. International Institutions

Formation, Purpose, Importance and Issues : Internation Institutions of Trade – WTO, UNCTAD, IMF, World Bank, ADB, Trade Blocks and Regional Economic Corporation – SAARC, European Union, BRICS, ASEAN

☞ ☞ ☞

Origin and Development of Global Business
BBA (IB) : (Sem. - II)

Question Paper Pattern (2019)

Q. No.	Compulsory / Choice	Name of the Question	Marks	Total Marks
1.	Compulsory Question	**Objective Type Question**		
		Multiple Choice Questions	5	
		Define the Terms	5	10
2.	Solve Any 1 Out of 2	Long Answer Question	1×10	10
2.	Solve Any 1 Out of 2	Long Answer Question	1×10	10
3.	Solve Any 4 Out of 5	Short Notes	4×5	20
				50 Marks

☞ ☞ ☞

Contents ...

1. **Industrial Development (Indian Context)** — 1.1 - 1.24

2. **National and International Trade** — 2.1 - 2.24

3. **Theories of International Trade** — 3.1 - 3.24

4. **International Institutions** — 4.1 - 4.32

• **Model Question Paper** — M.1 - M.2

Chapter **1** ...

Industrial Development
(Indian Context)

Contents ...

1.1   Globalization - The Concept and Importance
     1.1.1   Concept of Globalization
     1.1.2   Importance of Globalization in Modern World
     1.1.3   Advantages of Globalization
     1.1.4   Disadvantages of Globalization
1.2   Introduction to International Business
1.3   Difference between Domestic Business and International Business
1.4   Means of Entry into the International Business
     1.4.1   Imports and Exports
     1.4.2   Management Contract
     1.4.3   Franchising
     1.4.4   Licensing
     1.4.5   Contract Manufacturing
     1.4.6   Turnkey Project
     1.4.7   Wholly Owned Subsidiary (WOS)
     1.4.8   Joint Venture (JV)
     1.4.9   Mergers and Acquisition (M and A)
     1.4.10 Use of Logo
     1.4.11 Opening of Branch Offices
1.5   Industrialization - The Concept and Stages
     1.5.1   The Concept of Industrialization
     1.5.2   Phases of Industrialization (Industrial Revolution)
     •   Points to Remember
     •   Questions for Discussion

Learning Objectives ...

➢ To study the concept of globalization and its importance.

➢ To study the contribution of International and Domestic business for effective trading.

➢ To study the different facets of industrialization and its stages.

1.1 GLOBALIZATION - THE CONCEPT AND IMPORTANCE

The concept of marketing has evolved from a simple exchange transaction to a complex and complicated one, involving a number of interconnected and interrelated variables. As the concept of marketing has undergone a change, numerous definitions have been put forward by different thinkers at different intervals.

1.1.1 Concept of Globalization

Globalization is a term used to a more connected and interdependent world. Such a connected world facilitates spread of products, technology, information, and jobs across national borders and cultures. In economic terms, it describes an interdependence of nations around the world promoted through free trade. Globalization implies the incorporation of countries in the global economy through a network of international trade, production and finance. Basically, globalization has two major dimensions:

(i)   Globalization of markets.

(ii) Globalization of production.

Primarily, globalisation is seen as economic integration, achieved through the establishment of a global market place, which promotes free trade and has minimum regulations. Globalisation can also be viewed in terms of Internationalisation, as a harbinger of global peace and well-being of the entire world.

Fig. 1.1

Definitions:

1. According to **Albrow**, *"Globalization refers to all those processes by which the people of the world are incorporated into a single world society, global society."*

2. According to **Giddens**, *"Globalization can be defined as the intensification of worldwide social relations which link distant localities in such a way that local happenings are shaped by events occurring many miles away and vice versa."*

3. According to **Held**, *"Globalization refers to the widening, deepening and speeding up of global interconnectedness. Globalization can be thought of as a process (or set of processes) which embodies a transformation in the spatial organisation of social relations and transactions - assessed in terms of their extensity, intensity, velocity and impact - generating transcontinental or interregional flows, and networks of activity, interaction, and the exercise of power."*

4. According to **Hill**, *"Globalization is the shift towards a more integrated and interdependent world economy."*

Globalization has led to economic and social changes during its adventure. Management Guru Peter Drucker refers to Globalization as a "psychological phenomenon", citing how owning an automobile in China is now considered a necessity instead of a luxury. Globalization is actually a social, cultural, legal and political phenomenon. Socially, Globalization leads to greater interaction among citizens of different countries. Culturally, globalization epitomizes the exchange of ideas, values, and artistic expression among cultures. In fact, it aslo implies a trend toward the development of single global culture. Globalization has shifted attention to intergovernmental organizations like the World Trade Organization (WTO), World Bank (WB), IMF (International Monetary Fund), United Nations (UN) and the World Trade Organization (WTO) which support globalization and international trade. The defining perspective of globalization is "integration of the world".

Several scholars trace the beginning of Globalization to Columbus's voyage to the New World in 1492. It is true that people travelled to nearby and faraway places before Columbus's voyage as well and exchanged their ideas, products, and customs along the way. For instance, The Silk Road, an ancient network of trade routes across China, Central Asia, and the Mediterranean used between 50 B.C.E. and 250 C.E. cannot be ruled out.

Leaving history apart, Globalization gained pace since 1990's. Even India formally embraced glaobalization with LPG (Liberalization, Privatization and Globalization) as a part of economic reforms taken after the BOP (Balance of Payment) Crisis in 1991. With the Information Age reaching to developing coutries, globalization went into overdrive. Developments in computer and communications technology propelled a new global era and redefined what it meant to be connected. Today, the world economy has become interdependent to an extent that national independence is seen as an anachronism. This interdependence is driven by science, technology and the forces of modernity. Globalization has the potential to raise the standard of living in poor and less developed countries by providing job opportunity, modernization, technological proliferation and improved access to goods and services. However, it can destroy job opportunities in developed countries, especially the high-wage countries as the production of goods moves across borders, in search for cost-competitive labour. Still, a global free market has benefited large number of corporations in developed countries. Its impact remains mixed for workers, cultures, and small businesses around the world, in both developed and developing nations.

There are many ways of depicting globalisation, but one of the most vivid example is reflected in Princess Diana's death, which goes as follows:

"An English Princess with an Egyptian boyfriend, crashes in a French tunnel, driving a German car with a Dutch engine, driven by a Belgian who was high on Scottish whiskey, followed closely by Italian Paparazzi, on Japanese motorcycles, treated by an American doctor, using Brazilian medicines!

And this is sent to you by an Indian, using Bill Gates technology which he stole from the Japanese.

And you are probably reading this on one of the IBM clones that use Taiwanese-made chips, and Korean made monitors, assembled by Bangladeshi workers in a Singapore plant, transported by lorries driven by Pakistanis, hijacked by Indonesians and finally sold to you by the Chinese! "

The spread of Globalization can be attributed to the following:

1. Development in Transportation, with respect to the routes as well as the transportation medium, say, airplanes, railways, steamboats, cars etc.

2. ICT (Information Communication and Technology).

3. Spread of ideas about liberty, equality, and fraternity.

4. Industrialization.

5. Information Age.

6. Changes in the sphere of public policy.

There is a misconception that Globalisation affects only those businesses which deal in International trade. However, that is not true. Even a domestic business is affected by Globalisation, as it faces competition from global players and needs to adapt to new techniques and methods. For example, Indian electronics industry has been facing pricing pressures due to proliferation of Chinese goods. In the words of Drucker, "All institutions have to make global competitiveness a strategic goal. No institution can hope to survive, let alone succeed, unless it measures up to the standards set by the leaders in its field, anyplace in the world".

Real World Example of Globalization:

A car manufacturer based in Japan manufactures auto parts in several developing countries. These parts are then shipped to another country for assembly. Afterwards, the finished cars can be sold in any nation.

1.1.2 Importance of Globalization in Modern World

Globalization has played a major role in today's modern economy, on several fronts. These aspects are highlighted below:

1. Globalization has allowed developing countries to catch up to industrialized nations through technology transfer, increased manufacturing, diversification, and economic expansion

2. For developing countries, Globalization has led to improvements in standard of living

3. Gobalization provides tremendous advantage to multinational firms, as they already have the knowledge required to produce and to market goods and services internationally.

4. Corporations have been able to gain a competitive advantage on several fronts, thanks to globalization. These include reduction in operating costs by manufacturing at a location which has a cost-competitive labour, buying raw materials at a cheaper price due to reduction of tariffs

5. Globalization facilitates entry of several multinationals in a host country. As a result, people can have access to better products in terms of price and quality. Most importantly, they now have a choice and a voice.

6. Globalization provides a huge market size for multinational businesses. As a result, they can play in high volumes and reap the benefits of economies of scale.

7. Outsourcing by companies located in developed countries has resulted in jobs, prosperity and technology to developing countries. For instance, Indian IT sector firms such as Infosys, TCS, Wipro have nearly 70% of their revenues coming from USA and Europe. Their clients included Apple, Citi Bank, Microsoft, and several multinationals based in developed countries. These firms are reaping the advantage of Dollar earnings and Rupee expenses.

8. Globalization has advanced social justice on an international scale, and several International organizations such as United Nations have focused their attention on human rights and human welfare worldwide.

9. Developing countries such as India and China have reaped benefits in terms of increased GDP. Reduction in poverty, more of their citizens moving to middle class and higher middle class. China has served the world as a low-cost manufacturing hub with its cheap labour. On the other hand, India has emerged as a top outsourcing destination, especially for IT and accounting services.

10. Globalization has provided developing countries an access to the markets of developed countries, and developing countries can export cheap goods there.

11. Globalization has the potential to make this world a better place by solving some of the deep-rooted problems like unemployment and poverty

12. Free trade, a major component of globalization can provide a higher global economic growth, create jobs opportunities and make companies more competitive.

13. Globalization can provide poor countries an access to foreign capital and technology, thereby giving them a chance to develop economically and prosper.

1.1.3 Advantages of Globalization

1. Richer nations can support poorer nations in period of crisis.

2. Increasing diversity in many countries implies further opportunity to learn about and celebrate other cultures. The sense of a global village has emerged.

3. Corporations all over the world have the opportunity to gain access to millions of new consumers.

4. Globalization results in increased trade amongst nations.

5. For consumers, globalization leads to lower prices and better quality products. As a result of reduced prices, several products have become affordable for a lot of people in the world.

6. Globalization leads to a competition within domestic product, capital, and labour markets, as well as amongst the nations adopting different trade and investment strategies. This very competition can bring in higher output and increased productivity.

7. Increased trade can foster cordial relations between different countries in the world, thereby promoting global peace.

8. Globalization has been quite successful in lifting a large number of people out of poverty.

1.1.4 Disadvantages of Globalization

1. Increased risk for the transmission of diseases like ebola or severe acute respiratory syndrome (SARS)

2. Globalization can lead to the weakening of state sovereignty and state structures. In fact, Globalisation may indeed end the nation-state if the nation-state fails to redefine itself to meet the new conditions it faces in the global environment.

3. Economic downturn in one country can create spill-over effects on the world economy in general. This was evident through the 2008 global financial crisis, which started in USA and had a dominant effect on other parts of the world as well.

4. Globalization has resulted in a concentration of wealth and power in the hands of a small corporate elite only. Also, in case of developing countries, benefits of globalization have reached to a small fraction of population. In other words, rich are getting richer and the poor poorer

5. Globalization ignited debate in developed countries such as USA, for two major reasons:

   - Companies in USA employing migrant workers, as they come at a lower cost as compared to their USA counterparts.

   - Industries in USA shifting to new locations abroad, resulting in less job opportunities for its citizens

6. Cultural exchange facilitated by globalization has been largely a one-sided affair. Companies in developed countries are able to pass and impose their culture on to the citizens of developing countries. However, vice-versa is not happening.

7. Multinational corporations (MNC's) are accused of social injustice, unfair working conditions (less wages for labour alongwith deteriorating living and working conditions for them).

8. MNC's have hardly shown any concern for environment, and have been accused of mismanagement of natural resources, and ecological damage. They have also been found to influencing political decisions in the host country using their financial muscle.

1.2 INTRODUCTION TO INTERNATIONAL BUSINESS

Trade refers to the exchange of goods and services for money. The trade can happen within the geographical limits of a country, called as Domestic business. Alternatively, the trade can even take place beyond the boundaries of a country, or between two countries, which is referred to as International business. There are several privileges for a domestic business such as low transaction cost, less period between production and sale of goods, low transportation cost, Government schemes for small-scale enterprises, etc

Definition of International Business:

> According to **International Business Journal**, *"International business is a commercial enterprise that performs economical activity beyond the bounds of its location, has branches in two or more foreign countries and makes use of economic, cultural, political, legal and other differences between countries."*

Over the past two decades, there is an increasing trend of businesses venturing into international markets, thanks to advancement in ICT (Information and communications technology). Businessses have ventured into international markets in search of possible opportunities. These opportunities include bigger market for the firms, thereby increasing their sales and profitability Opportunities are also been provided in terms of business friendly environment, relaxed legal and taxation aspects, availability of high-skilled human resources, including cost-competitive labour force.

There is no doubt that International business is an extension of domestic business. Domestic business and International business do exhibit similarities in certain factors, such as –

1. Ensuring that customer's needs are satisfied.

2. Necessity of research and development.

3. Creation of goodwill through good quality products and ensuring proper after-sales service.

4. Marketing processes which consist of Product, Price, Place and Promotion.

However, undertaking international business is very complex as compared to managing and running a domestic business .The reasons are numerous. Different countries typically have different laws regarding trade and investment. Moreover, there are variations in business ethics and culture from country to country. Different political systems, monetary policies, geographical conditions, and currencies further add to complications. Hence, undertaking International business is much riskier and complicated as compared to domestic business. And these are all possible factors that could make international business more complicated and therefore, riskier than doing business at home. A business entity desirous of carrying out business in a different land will be faced with many such issues, making it potentially more difficult as compared to being domestic. Several other factors add to complications in doing International business including national wealth disparities, regional diversity, cultural diversity and population diversity. Even market characteristics such as demand pattern, channels of distribution, methods of promotion etc. varies from market to market. In brief, international business suffers from several obstacles like barrier to entry in the international market like tariffs and quota, political, socio- cultural, economic and other factors.

International business can range from exporting products in small quantities to forming strategic alliances in foreign countries, to a FDI (Foreign direct investment). International business encompasses all commercial activities to promote the transfer of goods, services, resources, people, ideas, and technologies across the borders. If a business concern wants to succeed in the international market, it needs to plan its business strategies as per the requirement of the foreign market Multi-national companies who have reaped huge success in the arena of international businesses recognize the diversity of the global marketplace and are able to deal with the uncertainties and risks of doing business in a continually changing global market.

International business management requires knowledge and skills above and beyond normal business expertise. These include :

(1) Familiarity with, and adherence to the business regulations of the nations in which the organization operates

(2) Deep understanding of local customs and traditions.

(3) Product quality and delivery specified by the standards of the respective nations.

(4) Capability to conduct business transactions involving multiple currencies.

Successful Corporations in International Business:

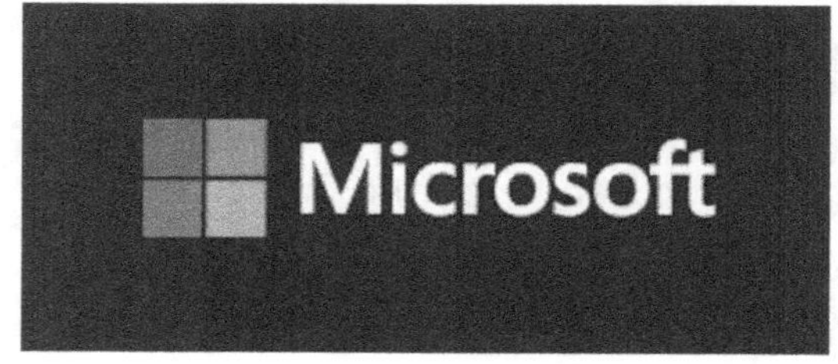

Fig. 1.2

1.3 DIFFERENCE BETWEEN DOMESTIC BUSINESS AND INTERNATIONAL BUSINESS

Domestic business is the one where buyer and seller are located in the same country and all manufacturing and trade takes place in a single country. In case of International business, the buyer and seller are located in different countries and manufacturing and trading operations can take place in several countries.

Domestic business and International business differ from each other in a variety of aspects. Given below are a few vital differences.

1. **Meaning and Scope:** Economic transactions of a Domestic business are confined to the geographical boundaries of a country. On the other hand, international business is not restricted to a single country. A firm carrying out international business is engaged in economic transactions with several countries in the world.

2. **Area of Operations:** The area of operation of the domestic business is limited to the home country. The area of operation of an international business is enormous, as it carries out its operations in many countries at the same time.

3. **Quality standards:** Doing international business requires adherence to high quality standards of products and services, which are set according to global standards. On the other hand, quality standards provided by a domestic business is comparatively low

4. **Size of Market:** International business offers opportunities in terms of huge market size. The company conducting international business can play high volume game and reap advantages of Economies of Scale. The same may not be easily possible for a company engaged in domestic business only, as the market size is limited.

5. **Currency Aspect:** Domestic business deals in a single currency, i.e. the currency of the country in which it operates. On the contrary, international business deals in the multiple currencies, and even involve exchanging them as per the exchange rates.

6. **Investment Requirements:** Capital investment required in international business is quite high as compared to domestic business.

7. **Restrictions – Regulations and Taxation:** International business deals with operations in several countries, and as a result, is subject to rules, regulations, and taxation policies of different countries, thereby inducing several restrictions on it. On the contrary, Domestic Business operates in one country only, and hence is subject to rules, regulations and taxation policies of a single country. International business also faces several barriers such as tariff and quotas

8. **Customer Characteristics:** Customers in a domestic business exhibit, more or less, similar characteristics in terms of their purchases, tastes, habits, preferences etc. Thus, the nature of customers is likewise, homogenous. In case of international business, these characteristics exhibited by customers differ from country to country and thus, display a heterogeneous nature.

9. **Geographical Distances:** In case of international business, geographical distances are huge as compared for domestic business. At times, geographic distances in case of International business is of several multiples of domestic business, thereby adding to trade execution time in case of International business.

10. **Mobility of Factors of Production:** In domestic business, factors of production, especially, labour and capital are easily mobile. However, in case of International business, the mobility of factors of production is restricted due to several geographical, political and legal aspects. As commented by Adam Smith, "Of all sorts of luggage, man is the most difficult to be transported".

11. **Taxation-Custom Duties:** Domestic business has to pay limited taxes such as GST (Goods and Service tax). International Business has to pay additional taxes such as Customs duties (Import duty) and CVD (Countervailing duty).

Given below is a snapshot showing the differences between Domestic business and International business.

	Basis	Domestic Business	International Business
1.	**Business area:**	Domestic business takes place within the geographical boundaries of a country.	International business occurs between 2 different countries, i.e. it is cross-border.
2.	**Location of buyer and seller:**	Buyer and seller are located in the same country.	Buyer and seller are located in different countries.
3.	**Movement of factors of production:**	Easily mobile.	It is difficult to move factors of production beyond borders.
4.	**Currency:**	A single currency is used.	Multiple currencies are used (or exchanged for economic transactions).
5.	**Culture:**	The market culture is relatively uniform across the regions within a country.	The market culture widely differs amongst different nations.
6.	**Risk factor:**	Less as compared to International business.	High risk factor.
7.	**Rules and regulations:**	Rules and regulations of the county of incorporation are applicable.	International regulations as well as host country regulations are applicable.
8.	**Size of market:**	Relatively less as compared to International business.	Huge market size and opportunities exist.
9.	**Restrictions on businesses:**	Few restrictions exist in case of Domestic business.	Many restrictions apply in case of international business.
10.	**Investment requirement:**	Lower.	Generally high.
11.	**Business exposure:**	Very little experience or exposure.	Companies doing International business have perfected principles, procedures and practices at international level.
12.	**Level of competition:**	Less as compared to International business.	Dynamic and complex competition.

... (Contd.)

Basis	Domestic Business	International Business
13. Tariffs and customs duties:	Not applicable.	Applicable.
14. Geographical distances:	Short as compared to International business.	Long distances.
15. Transportation costs:	Lower as compared to International business.	Generally quite high as compared to domestic business.
16. Custom duties:	No custom duties applicable.	Import duty and CVD is to be paid in case of International business.
17. Transaction time:	Quick business is possible due to less distance and restrictions.	More transaction time required due to geographical distances and certain regulatory compliances.
18. Economies of scale:	Economies of scale may not be achieved due to limited volumes.	Economies of scale can be achieved due to advantages of high volumes.

1.4 MEANS OF ENTRY INTO THE INTERNATIONAL BUSINESS

Nowadays, many corporates are looking to expand into countries other than their own. The obvious reasons are expansion of market, increased sales, economies of scale and international brand image. However there are various nuances in dealing new markets and modes of entrance. Hence this requires a careful strategy to be crafted, if one wants to be successful.

Business can enter the global market by selling immediately to customers in export territories, marketing products through a local distributor, taking part in a joint venture. The decision of mode of entry depends on the following factors:

(1) Ownership,

(2) Location,

(3) Internationalisation advantages in terms of efficiency, costs, and technology.

The various strategies used for gaining entry into International business are as shown in figure below:

Fig. 1.3

1.4.1 Imports and Exports

Imports and exports is amongst the most commonly used method to gain access to International market. This serves as the very foundation for International business. Imports refer to purchasing of goods from a supplier in another country, whereas, export means selling of goods to a buyer in a foreign country.

1.4.2 Management Contract

- As per the Business dictionary definition, a management contract is an agreement between investors or owners of a project, and a management company hired for coordinating and overseeing a contract. It spells out the conditions and duration of the agreement, and the method of computing management fees.

- Management contract is thus, an agreement between two companies, wherein one company provides managerial assistance, technical expertise and specialized services to another company for a certain period in return for monetary compensation.

- A management contract is an arrangement under which operational control of an enterprise is vested by contract in a separate enterprise that performs the necessary managerial functions in return for a fee. The seller provides management skills and technological skills. Partners own the production facilities. Management contracts thus, involve not just selling a method of doing things, as is the case   with franchising or licensing, but involve actually doing them.

- A management contract can include a wide range of activities, such as technical operation of a production facility, management of personnel, accounting, marketing services and training.

- In Asia, many hotels operate under management contract arrangements, as they can more easily obtain economies of scale, a global reservation systems, brand recognition etc. These contracts are signed for a period, as high as 30 years, and having a fee as high as 3% of total revenues and 5-10% of gross operating profit.

- Management contracts have been widely used in airline industry and hotels. It has been used especially when foreign government action restricts other entry methods. lack of local skills to run a project can also lead to formation of management contracts. It is an alternative to foreign direct investment as it does not involve as high risk and can yield higher returns for the company.

Advantages:

(i) A company earns additional income without undertaking any additional investment.

(ii) Enhances company's image in front of investors.

(iii) Helps the company enter business areas in another country.

Disadvantages:

(i) Possibilty of leak of technology and other secrets.

(ii) Can spoil company's brand name if the company in host country does not maintain the quality standards.

1.4.3 Franchising

- Franchising can be called a kind of licensing. The franchising system can be defined as: "A system in which semi-independent business owners (franchisees) pay fees and royalties to a parent company (franchiser) in return for the right to become identified with its trademark, to sell its products or services, and often to use its business format and system."

- Franchising involves two parties:

(i) Franchisor,   (ii) Franchisee.

- As per **Doole & Lowe, 2008,** the franchisor is the owners of the business format who issues a licence through an agreement which allows the franchisee the right or privilege to distribute the goods and services that represents the franchisor's brand and business system for an agreed sum (royalty or fee).

- A franchiser grants a franchisee the right to use of a brand-name identity within a geographic area, but retains control over pricing, marketing, and standardized service norms.

- Franchising is limited to trademarks and operating know-how of the business.

- McDonalds which happens to be one of the largest food service companies in the world, has entered various international markets through franchising.

Advantages of the international franchising mode:

(i) Low political risk

(ii) Low cost

(iii) Splits the investment risk

(iv) Increases the opportunity to locate product distribution channels

(v) Allows simultaneous expansion into different regions of the world

(vi) Well selected partners bring financial investment as well as managerial capabilities to the operation.

Disadvantages of international franchising mode:

(i) Maintaining control over franchisee may be difficult.

(ii) Conflicts with franchisee are likely, including legal disputes.

(iii) Preserving franchisor's image in the foreign market may be challenging.

(iv) Requires monitoring and evaluating performance of franchisees, and providing ongoing assistance.

(v) Franchisees may take advantage of acquired knowledge and become competitors/conendors in the future.

(vi) Less demand when starting to franchise a company can result in wrong selection.

(vii) Selection of a wrong franchisee can ruin the company's name and reputation in the market place.

(viii) International franchising requires a bigger financial investment to attract prospects and support and manage franchises as compared to other styles such as exporting and licensing.

1.4.4 Licensing

- Licensing refers to a contractual arrangement, wherein, one firm sells access to its patents, trade secrets, or technology to another firm for a fixed sum and sales royalties (2% - 5%).

- Thus, the firm, called the licensor, leases the right to use its intellectual property— technology, work methods, patents, copyrights, brand names, or trademarks—to another firm, called the licensee, in return for a fee.

- In a licensing agreement, the licensor gives something of value to the licensee in exchange for certain performance and payments from the licensee. It should always be formalized in a written document.

- The property licensed can include one or more of the following:
    - Patents
    - Trademarks
    - Copyrights
    - Technology
    - Technical know-how
    - Specific business skills

Advantages of Licensing:

(i) Low financial risks.

(ii) Low-cost method to assess market potential.

(iii) Avoid tariffs, Non tariff barriers and restrictions on foreign investment.

(iv) Helps to avoid host country regulations applicable to equity ventures.

(v) Licensee provides knowledge of local markets.

Disadvantages of Licensing:

(i) Limited market opportunities and thereby limited profits.

(ii) A very limited form of foreign market participation.

(iii) Dependence on licensee.

(iv) Potential conflicts with licensee.

(v) Possibility of licensee becoming a future competitor.

Difference between Franchising and Licensing:

Licensing is a relatively sophisticated arrangement where a firm transfers the rights to the use of a product or service to another firm. It is a particularly useful strategy if the purchaser of the license has a relatively large market share in the market that is targeted for entry. Licenses can be for marketing or production. A licensee does not hold the rights to the trademark and logo of the parent company's brand as the franchisee does. Licensees also do not receive the same extent of support and training as compared to a franchisee. Licensing costs much lesser in terms of the initial investment and ongoing charges. A franchising business requires a franchisee to pay royalty every time a profit is made. On the other hand, for a licensee, no such expense is demanded.

Franchising is a typical process for rapid market expansion. Franchising works well for firms that have a repeatable business model (food outlets) that can be easily transferred into other markets. Franchising is a recognized legal terminology, in the sense that it subjects the party offering these services to certain rules and regulations, whereas, licensing generally does not come with these issues.

1.4.5 Contract Manufacturing

- Contract manufacturing refers to outsourcing entire or part of manufacturing operations. Promotion and distribution is controlled by the company.

- Contract manufacturing is common in case of pharmaceuticals and Personal Care products.

- For example, the iPad and iPhone, which are products from Apple Inc., are manufactured in China by Foxconn. Here, Foxconn can be termed as a contract manufacturer and Apple benefits from a lower cost of manufacturing devices

1.4.6 Turnkey Project

- A turnkey project refers to a contract under which a firm agrees to fully design, construct and equip a manufacturing/business/service facility and turn the project over to the purchaser when its ready for operation, in return for some remuneration.

- Several airports, dams, roads, electric power stations, refineries, chemical plants and automobile plants have been built through turnkey projects.

1.4.7 Wholly Owned Subsidiary (WOS)

- Wholly owned subsidiary can mean building a new plant (Greenfield Investment), like Volkswagen India or acquire a going concern (Brownfield Investment).

- It can also involve to purchase distributor, to obtain a distribution network familiar with products.

- In a wholly owned subsidiary, the firm owns 100 percent of the stock.

1.4.8 Joint Venture (JV)

- Joint venture refers to a cooperative effort among two or more organizations that share common interest in business enterprise. Each party to a joint venture contributes assets, has some equity, and shares risk.

- The key to a joint venture is the sharing of a common business objective Joint venture means a corporate entity formed by international company and local owners for doing business. A joint venture can also be formed by two international companies for the purpose of doing business in a third market.

- This mode of entry is usually adopted by MNC's to enter into foreign markets. For example, DCM Group and Daewoo Motors entered into a joint venture to form DCM Daewoo Limited to manufacture automobiles in India.

- The venture can be for one specific project only or a continuing business relationship. For example, Sony-Ericsson is a joint venture between Japanese consumer electronics company Sony Corporation and the Swedish telecommunications company Ericsson to make mobile phones.

1.4.9 Mergers and Acquisition (M and A)

- Merger refers to two or more companies combining their operations into a single entity. For example, Hindustan Computers Ltd., Hindustan Instruments Ltd., Indian Software Co. Ltd and Indian Reprographic Ltd merged to form Hindustan Computers Ltd. (HCL).

- Acquisition refers to an act of acquiring effective control by one company over assets or management of another company. In an acquisition, one company purchases another company. For example, Tata Steel acquired Corus Group PLc., UK.

- A company can enter international markets through mergers and acquisitions, via purchasing a foreign company, acquiring control over its assets or management.

- Mergers and acquisitions provide easy and instant entry into global business. For example, Tata Motors entered UK market through purchase of Jaguar and Landrover.

Advantages:

(i) Immediate ownership and control.

(ii) Easy way of entering international markets.

(iii) Diversification of markets.

(iv) Companies in developed countries can tap the potential in emerging economies.

Disadvantages:

(i) Acquiring a firm in a foreign country is a complex task, which involves dealing with various legal and regulatory issues in both the countries.

(ii) An acquired company's problems related to debt and labour will have to be dealt with.

1.4.10 Use of Logo

Use of logo is an important sign of branding the product or service of the company in an international market. It serves to capture the attention of the market. Use of logo should reflect the corporate identity in international market.

Logos of Few Successful MNC's:

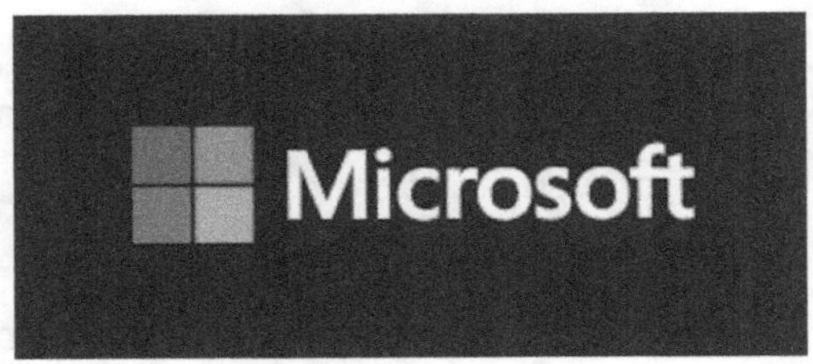

Fig. 1.4

1.4.11 Opening of Branch Offices

- A company can enter international business by opening its branches in foreign countries.
- Through these branches, it can get a feel of that county's market. It can then expand business into that country by opening more branches, or other modes.
- One can typically see banks expanding their branches in foreign countries.

For example, Citibank, Standard Chartered Bank etc.

1.5 INDUSTRIALIZATION - THE CONCEPT AND STAGES

1.5.1 The Concept of Industrialization

Industrialization is the process through which an economy is transformed from agricultural to one based on mass manufacturing of goods. In other words, Industrialization involves social and economic change that transforms human civilization from an agrarian society into an industrial society, involving the extensive re-organisation of an economy for the purpose of manufacturing. Industrialization thus implies the large-scale introduction of manufacturing into a society.

Industrialization empowers human beings to do more with less. Instead of taking days to plough a field with one horse, tractor can now be used to plough the field in a couple of hours. This frees up a man's time to do more work around the farm, and maybe even take a vacation, and spend quality time with family.

Definitions:

1. According to **International Encyclopedia of the Social and Behavioral Sciences,** *"Industrialization is the process of applying mechanical, chemical, and electrical sciences to reorganize production with inanimate sources of energy".*

2. According to **Ekpo**, *"Industrialization involves transformation of raw materials, with the aid of human resources and capital goods into consumers' goods (including food) and new capital goods".*

Features of Industrialization:

1. Replacement of manual labour by mechanized mass production.
2. Replacement of craftsmen assembly lines.
3. Increased economic growth and income of people.
4. Improved standard of living.
5. Efficient division of labour.
6. Use of technological innovation to solve problems.

Closely associated with Industrialization is the term 'Industrial Revolution', which indicated first transformation from an agricultural to an industrial economy. Industrial Revolution occurred during the 18th and 19th century in certain areas in Europe and North America, and later spread to other parts of the world.

1.5.2 Phases of Industrialization (Industrial Revolution)

According to Schwab, Industrial revolution implies the appearance of "new technologies and novel ways of perceiving the world that trigger a profound change in economic and social structures. According to World Economic Forum's report entitled, we are in the midst of a fourth phase of industrial revolution, with technology rapidly developing in areas like 3D printing, robotics and artificial intelligence.

We will see in brief the 4 phases of Industrial revolution.

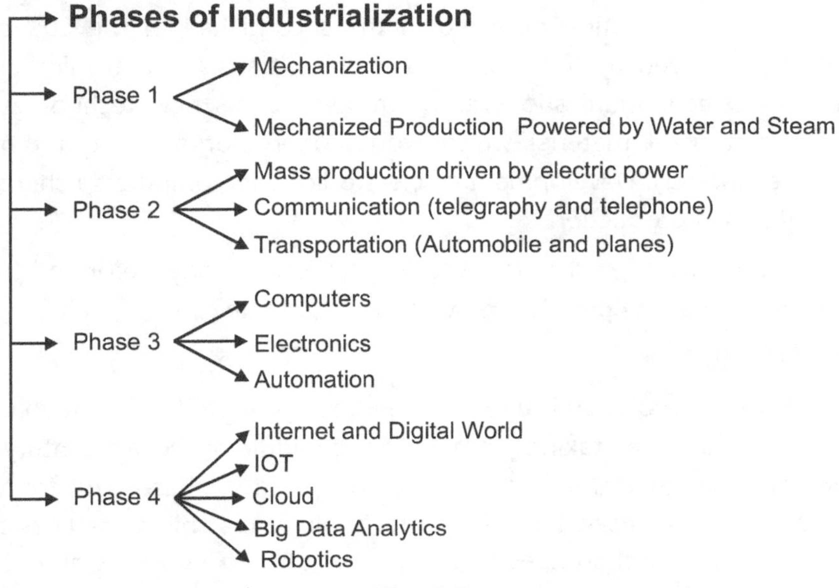

Fig. 1.5

Phase 1: (Mechanization)

The first phase of Industrial revolution spans from the end of the 18th century to the beginning of the 19th century. The distinguishing feature of this phase was mechanization, a process that replaced agriculture with industry as the foundations of the economic structure of society. With the invention of the steam engine, water and steam were used to mechanize production. Key inventions such as forging and new know-how in metal shaping gradually drew up the blueprints for the first factories and cities.

Human life took a shift from farm to all about the factory, and people moved from the country into town with the introduction of mechanical production.

Phase 2: (Electric Energy and Mass Production)

The second phase of Industrial revolution started towards the end of the 19th century. The phase was characterized emergence of a new source of energy: electricity, gas and oil. electric energy facilitated mass production. Capital structured around an economic and industrial model based on new "large factories", powered by the assembly line. The discovery of electricity and mass production fundamentally changed the way people lived and worked.

Even the steel industry began to develop and demand for steel grew exponentially. Chemical synthesis also developed to bring synthetic fabric, dyes and fertilizer to mankind.

Communication developed to a vast extent, thanks to the invention of the telegraph and the telephone as well as with the transportation methods, particularly the arrival of the automobile and the plane at the beginning of the 20th century.

Phase 3 (Electronics, Telecommunications and Computers)

The third Industrial revolution occurred in the second half of the 20th century. This revolution was characterized by the Rise of electronics (transistor and microprocessor), as well as the rise of telecommunications and computers. This new technology led to the production of miniaturized material which would open doors, most notably to space research and biotechnology. Development of electronics and computers ushered an era of high-level automation in production.

Computers, along with electronics and digital technology reformed nearly every industry, transforming the way people live, work, and communicate.

Phase 4 (Digital Revolution)

The fourth industrial revolution is underway and builds upon the third revolution and the digital revolution that has been taking place since the middle of the last century. Emergence of the **Internet** and digital world is a chief feature of this phase. The fourth industrial revolution is mainly characterized by merging technology that blurs the lines between the physical, digital and biological spheres to completely uproot industries all over the world. This includes transformations to entire production, management and governance systems.

The industry of today and tomorrow aim to connect all production means to enable their interaction in real time. Thanks to technologies such as the **Cloud**, Big Data Analytics and the IOT (Internet of Things), Factories 4.0 make communication among the different players and connected objects in a production line possible.

Other super features of Industry 4.0 include:
- Improved decision-making in real time.
- Anticipating inventory based on production.
- Improved coordination among jobs.
- Predictive maintenance, etc.
- Smart cities and powered by renewable sources of energy such as wind, and solar.
- Artificial intelligence (AI).
- Increasing computing power and data.
- Robotics.
- Drones.
- Virtual reality.
- Augmented reality.

Points to Remember

1. Globalization is the shift towards a more integrated and interdependent world economy.
2. International business can range from exporting products in small quantities to forming strategic alliances in foreign countries to a FDI.

3. The importance means of entry into the international business are as follows :
   - (a) Imports and exports
   - (b) Management contracts
   - (c) Franchising
   - (d) Licensing
   - (e) Contract manufacturing
   - (f) Turn key projects
   - (g) Wholly owned subsidiaries
   - (h) Joint Venture
   - (i) Mergers and acquisitions
   - (j) Use of logo
   - (k) Opening of branch offices.
4. The four phases of industrialization are as follows :
   - (a) Phase 1 : (Mechanization).
   - (b) Phase 2 : (Electric Energy and Mass Production).
   - (c) Phase 3 : (Electronics, Telecommunications and Computers).
   - (d) Phase 4 : (Digital revolution).

Questions for Discussion

1. What do you mean by Globalization? Explain the significance (importance) of globalization.
2. What is Globalization? Explain the advantages and disadvantages of Globalization.
3. What do you mean by International Business?
4. Explain the various means of entry into International business.
5. Elucidate the difference between National business (Domestic business) and International Business.
6. What is Industrialization? Explain the various phases (stages) of Industrialization (industrial revolution).

Write short notes on :

1. Export	2. Import
3. International Business	4. Globalization
5. Industrialization	6. Mergers and Acquisitions
7. Licensing	8. Franchising
9. Logo	10. Management Contract
11. Joint Venture	12. Management Contract
13. Wholly owned subsidiary	14. Globalization

Multiple Choice Questions:

1. Globalization refers to ......
   - (a) A more integrated world
   - (b) Global Warming
   - (c) Closed Domain
   - (d) None of these
2. Which is not an advantage of international trade?
   - (a) Export of surplus production
   - (b) Import of defence material
   - (c) Dependence on foreign countries
   - (d) Availability of cheap raw material
3. Globalization can create problems for business because ......
   - (a) It can result in more competition.
   - (b) It reduces vulnerability to political risk and uncertainty when operating abroad.
   - (c) It means that they can increase prices.

    (d) All of the options given are correct.

4. What refers to a contractual arrangement, wherein, one firm sells access to its patents, trade secrets, or technology to another firm for a fixed sum and sales royalties?
   - (a) Franchise
   - (b) Joint Venture
   - (c) Licensing
   - (d) Management Contract

5. The third phase of industrial revolution was characterized by ......
   - (a) Electronics
   - (b) Mass Production
   - (c) Mechanisation
   - (d) None of these

6. Trade that takes place within the geographical boundaries of a country ......
   - (a) International Trade
   - (b) Domestic Trade
   - (c) Global Trade
   - (d) Cross Border Trade

7. Which of the following is the best explanation of a joint venture?
   - (a) A general business partnership.
   - (b) The merging of two or more businesses to pursue a business venture.
   - (c) A partnership of businesses formed to engage in a short term business venture together.
   - (d) A business supplying raw materials to another business.

Answer to MCQ's

(1) – (a), (2) – (c), (3) – (a), (4) – (c), (5) – (a), (6) – (b), (7) – (b)

Chapter **2**...

National and International Trade

Contents ...

2.1   Concept of Trade - National Trade and International Trade
    2.1.1   Introduction to Trade
    2.1.2   Concept of National Trade
    2.1.3   Contribution of National Trade
    2.1.4   Concept of International Trade
    2.1.5   Contribution of International Trade
2.2   Components of National Business (Environment)
2.3   Components of International Business (Environment)
2.4   PESTEL Model (Political, Economic, Social, Technological, Environmental and Legal)
    2.4.1   PESTEL Model
    2.4.2   Performing PESTEL Analysis – The Steps
    2.4.3   Importance of PESTEL Analysis
2.5   Geographical Indication (GI)
    2.5.1   Concept of GI
    2.5.2   Nature of GI
    2.5.3   Importance of GI
    • Points to Remember
    • Questions for Discussion

Learning Objectives ...

➢ To understand the concept of national and international trade

➢ To understand the contribution of national trade and international trade to modern business

➢ To study the components of National Business (Environment)

➢ To study the components of International Business (Environment)

➢ To study the PESTEL model-Political, Economic, Social, Technological, Environmental and Legal factors related to Business

➢ To understand the importance of PESTEL model for a business venture

➢ To study the concept of GI (Geographical Indication) and its importance for a region

2.1 | CONCEPT OF TRADE - NATIONAL TRADE AND INTERNATIONAL TRADE

2.1.1 Introduction to Trade

Trade refers to buying and selling of goods and services for money or an equivalent of money. In other words, transfer or exchange of goods and services takes place in lieu of money.

Trade leads to satisfaction of human wants. Trade is conducted for earning profit, and to provide service to the consumers. Trade started with the beginning of human life and shall continue till its existence. Trade is an important social activity which helps to enhance the standard of living of consumers. Thus we can say that trade is a very important social activity.

Trade is broadly classified into following two types:

(i)   National trade, or Internal trade or Domestic trade.

(ii) International trade, or Foreign trade.

Trade	
National Trade **(Domestic Trade)**	**International Trade** **(Foreign Trade)**
Buyer and seller in same country.	Buyer and seller in different countries.
Trade within geographical borders.	Trade across geographical borders.

2.1.2 Concept of National Trade

National trade is also called as Internal trade or Domestic trade or Home trade. National trade involves exchange of domestic goods within the geographical boundaries of a country. For example, trade carried on among traders of Mumbai, Pune etc. is called National trade.

National trade can be further sub-divided into two categories:

(i) Wholesale Trade: In case of wholesale trade, large quantities are bought from producers or manufacturers and sold in lots to retailers for resale to consumers. The wholesaler is thus an intermediary, who serves as a link between manufacturer and retailer.

(ii) Retail Trade : A retailer buys quantities in smaller lots from the wholesalers and sells it in very small quantities to the consumers for personal use. The retailer is the last link in the distribution chain, who serves as a link between wholesalers and consumers.

2.1.3 Contribution of National Trade

National trade or Domestic trade is an important aspect of human life, as it leads to satisfaction of human wants and serves as an occupation. Major benefits arising from national trade are described below:

* National trade facilitates exchange of goods within the country, as it ensures that factors of production reach to the right places.

- National trade contributes to the growth of the economy, particularly with increase in consumption.
- National trade facilitates goods and services to reach to all parts of the country.
- National trade improves the standard of living of the citizens of the country
- National trade helps in creating employment opportunities in the country.
- National trade facilitates Industrial growth, by ensuring supply of raw materials.
- Though imports and exports are important from the economic viewpoint, a large portion of GDP contribution comes from internal trade.
- India's economic growth in recent years has been driven mainly by domestic demand, and Internal trade helps in meeting this demand.

2.1.4 Concept of International Trade

- Also known as External trade, or Foreign trade, International trade refers to buying and selling of goods and services between individuals or corporates of two or more countries. For example, Mr. A, a trader from Pune, sells his goods to Mr. B, a trader from Dubai.
- International trade, thus involves, economic exchange of goods and services between individuals/corporates/Governments of different countries.
- The direction of International trade is determined by the law of comparative advantage, which states that some markets hold specific advantages that allow them to generate products and services at a lower opportunity cost than others.
- International trade has grown rapidly over the past two decades, thanks to advances in ICT (Information Communication and Technology).
- International trade can be further sub-divided into three types:
  1. Export Trade.
  2. Import Trade.
  3. Entrepot Trade.

International Trade		
Export Trade	**Import Trade**	**Entrepot Trade**
• Sell goods to a foreign buyer.	• Purchase of goods from a foreign seller.	• Re-exports.
• Goods produced domestically.	• Goods produced in foreign country.	

Export Trade :

- In case of an Export trade, corporation from home country sells their goods to a corporation located in another country. For example, a trader from India sells his goods to a trader located in China.

- Export trade involves sale of goods and services to a buyer located in a foreign country. The goods produced in a home country are shipped from the port of the home country to a foreign country.

- Exports include merchandise exports (goods) as well as service exports (invisibles).

Import Trade :

- Imports involve purchase of goods and services from another country, in return for foreign exchange. In other words, Imports represent the inflow of goods and services into a country's market for consumption.

- The goods imported are not produced in the home country.

- The buyer of these goods and/or services is referred to as an "importer" and is based in the country of import.

Entrepot Trade :

- In an Entrepot trade, the goods are imported in a country with the sole purpose of re-exporting them to some another country. As a result, a trader conducting Entrepot trade becomes both the importer and the exporter for these goods.

- In an entrepot trade, the goods imported into a country are re-exported. The package does not undergo any repackaging or additional processing. Even if processing is done, it is minimal.

- Origins - *entry port trade* (avoids the payment of any import or export duties when the package is sent out from that port). Entrepot is mainly used to refer to duty-free ports having high volume of re-export trade.

- For example, if an Indian company were to import food grains from Bangladesh and export it immediately to USA, this would be called entrêpot trade for India.

2.1.5 Contribution of International Trade

International trade has helped create several bridges between producers and consumers across the globe. Increasing international trade is vital to the continuance of globalisation. Without International trade, the goods and services available to the consumers will be limited to those produced within their own borders. International trade helps economies all over the world via several aspects as mentioned below:

- International trade has contributed to rise in living standards, particularly in case of developing economies.

- International trade provides employment opportunities for people all over the world.

- International trade gives the power of 'Choice' to the consumers, and helps them to enjoy a larger variety of goods.

- In recent years, International trade is occupying a larger share of GDP for many countries.

- International trade helps countries abundant in natural endowments to make use of them, and benefit from them. For example, oil rich countries like Saudi Arabia, Iran, Qatar can export oil, thanks to International trade.

- International trade helps countries to pursue specialisation and this enables companies to benefit from economies of scale.

- For the corporates, International trade provides them a huge market size, in the form of consumers in different countries.

- International trade results in improved efficiencies, as a result of competition emanating from companies located in other countries.

- With International trade, consumers benefit as they can have access to better quality products.

- International trade facilitates consumers to get those goods that can't be produced in the home country.

- International trade provides for flow of technology, which allows for rise in productivity.

- With increased competition in the market, price for consumer goods can decline, making it affordable for more number of consumers.

- International trade helps in sharing of best management practices

- International trade has been an important factor in global development and economic growth. This growth been especially visible in Asian countries, with raising GDP and reduction in poverty.

- International trade results in peaceful and cordial relations between the trading partners.

2.2 COMPONENTS OF NATIONAL BUSINESS (ENVIRONMENT)

National business, also known as Domestic business, operates within the geographical borders of a country. Here, the buyer and seller are located in the same country and several business operations as well as execution of trade takes place in a single country.

Business environment is the aggregate of all conditions, events and influences that surround and affect it. The business environment is uncertain, and constantly changing.

Components of national business (environment) are basically divided into 2 broad categories:

1. Internal Environment

2. External Environment

Components of National Business (Environment)	
Internal Environment	**External Environment**
Factors within an organization.	Factors outside the business.
Controllable factors.	Factors beyond the control of business.

1. Internal Environment:

Internal environment is composed of multiple elements existing within (inside) an organization. It is true that Internal factors affect the functioning of the organization. However, these factors are mostly controllable, which implies that the organization can modify or adjust such factors. Internal environment broadly encompasses management, employees and corporate culture.

Some of the important internal factors are:

(i) Financial Capability: Financial capability refers to the availability, usage and management of funds. It also includes all related aspects that influence an organization's ability to implement its strategies.

Financial capability of an organization includes:

(a) Aspects related to the procurement of funds like various sources of finance, capital structure, financing pattern, working capital, debt, reserves and surplus.

(b) Aspects related to utility of funds such as capital investment, acquisition of fixed assets, current assets, and distribution of dividends

(c) Aspects related to management of funds like financial accounting and budgeting, management control system, financial health, cash, risk and return management, cost reduction and control, and tax planning.

(ii) Marketing Capability: Marketing capability factors relate to the marketing aspects, particularly the 4 P's of marketing (product, price, place or distribution of products, and promotion). Even the aspects of segmentation of market, quality, packaging. target market, advertising and company's overall positioning in the market is considered.

(iii) Operations Capability: Operations capability factors mainly deals with the production of the products or services, and use of material resources. Aspects related to the production system like capacity, location, layout, service, design, work system, degree of automation, aggregate production planning, material supply, as well as R & D system level of technology used, technical support etc. are the matter of concern.

(iv) Personnel Capability: These aspects focus on human resources in the organization. Aspects related to manpower, planning, selection, development of skills, training, compensation, appraisal, working conditions, employee satisfaction etc. are primarily dealt.

(v) Management Capability: Management capability relates to the integration, coordination and direction of the functional capabilities towards common organization's ability to implement its strategies is also determined by the very capability of its management.

Strategy formulation, mission, purpose and objective setting, management information system, corporate planning system are the important aspects of management capability.

2. External Environment:

External environment refers to factors that happen outside the business. External environment has an indirect influence on the business and includes factors beyond the control of the business.

External environment of a business consists of:

(i) Micro-environment, and

(ii) Macro-environment.

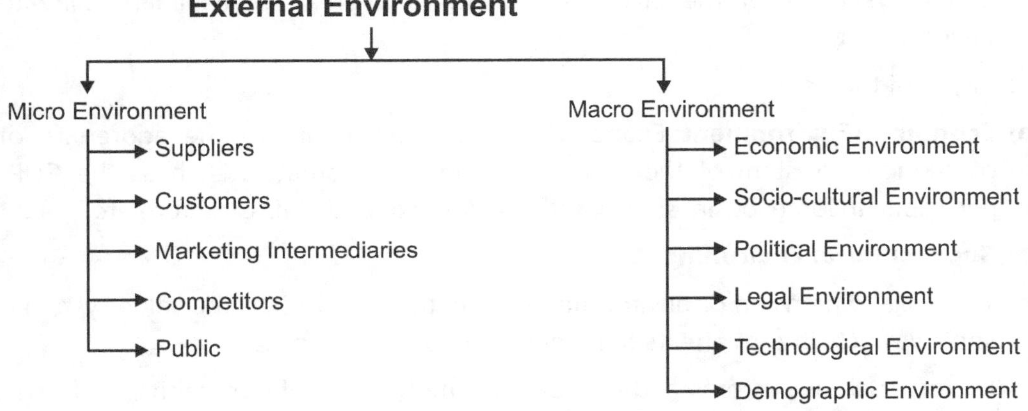

Fig. 2.1

(i) Micro Environment: The micro environment is known as the operating environment, or the task environment. The micro environmental forces have a direct bearing on the operations of the firm.

It consists of the following:

(a) Suppliers: It refers to entities who supply the inputs like raw materials and components to the company. Good relationships with suppliers are essential to get the right goods at right time.

(b) Customers: The major task of a business is to create new customers and get repeat visits and orders from its existing customers. A business exists as long as the customers purchase from the business.

(c) Marketing Intermediaries: The marketing intermediaries comprise of middlemen such as agents and merchants that help the company find customers or close sales. They include wholesalers, distributors, retailers etc.

(d) Competitors :

- A firm's competitors consists mainly of the other firms which market the same or similar products. However, with changing business dynamics, competitors also include other firms who compete for the income of the consumers.

- A firm's product, pricing, promotion and distribution strategies are influenced by the existing and anticipated competition.

(e) Public: Public can be believed of, as any group that has an actual or potential interest in or on an organization's ability to achieve its interest. Public basically includes citizens and media.

(ii) Macro Environment:

- Macro environment is also known as General environment and consists of larger societal forces that affect all the factors in company's micro environment.

- Macro factors are generally more uncontrollable than micro environment factors, and the success of the business depend to a great on its adaptability to the environment.

It consists of the below:

(a) Economic Environment: Economic environment refers to the aggregate of the nature of economic system of the country, economic parameters such as the GDP of a nation, per-capita income, business cycles, the socio-economic infrastructure etc.

(b) Socio-cultural Environment:

- The social dimension or environment of a nation determines the value system of the society which, in turn affects the functioning of the business.

- Factors such as customs and conventions, mobility of labour, habits, preferences of people etc. are included in Socio-cultural Environment

- All these factors have far-reaching impact on the business.

(c) Political Environment:

- It includes legislature, executive and judiciary.

- The political environment of a country is influenced by the political organizations, philosophy of political parties, ideology of government or party in power, nature and extent of bureaucracy influence of primary groups etc. influence the conduct of business

(d) Legal Environment:

- A business has to function within the framework of law.

- Legal environment refers to the actual laws, flexibility and adaptability of law and other legal rules and regulations governing the business. It may include the exact rulings and decision of the courts on business matters.

(e) Technological Environment:

- The technology adopted by the industries determines the type and quality of goods and services to be produced and the type and quality of plant and equipment to be used.

- Rapid changes in technologies influence business to a great extent.

(f) Demographic Environment : It refers to the characteristics of population in area such as age, income, educational attainment, asset ownership, employment status.

Size and growth rates of population, composition of population, family size, educational levels, economic stratification of the population, language, caste, religion, and location are also considered herein.

Analysis of these factors reveal the following:

(i)   Attractiveness of the market.

(ii) Suggests the type of products and services which will be demanded.

(iii) Pricing and promotional strategies.

(iv) Availability of skilled workforce, if operations are set up in this market.

2.3 COMPONENTS OF INTERNATIONAL BUSINESS (ENVIRONMENT)

International business involves a business activity that crosses national borders. It means that an organization buys and/or sells goods and services across two or more countries.

Similar to National trade, International trade has to take place taking a view of Macro-economic and Micro-economic parameters. However, International business has a wide scope, and hence some components are added. Major components of International business are detailed below:

1. International trade

2. Countertrade

3. Imports

4. Exports

5. Entrepot

6. Multinational Corporations

7. International business law

8. Trade agreements

9. Intellectual Property Rights(IPR)

10. International Finance

1. International Trade:

- International trade refers to the economic exchange of goods and services between individuals/corporates/Governments of different countries.

- The direction of International trade is determined by the law of comparative advantage, which states that some markets hold specific advantages that allow them to generate products and services at a lower opportunity cost than others.

- In the past two decades, advances in ICT (Information Communication and Technology) have resulted in exponential growth of International trade.

2. **Countertrade**
   - Countertrade involves exchange of goods or services for other goods or services. Countertrade is an exchange system in which goods and services are used in lieu of payment, instead of using money for this purpose.
   - For example, in the year 2000, India and Iraq agreed to exchange "oil for wheat and rice"

3. **Imports:**
   - Imports involve purchase of goods and services from another country, in return for foreign exchange. In other words, Imports represent the inflow of goods and services into a country's market for consumption.
   - The buyer of these goods and/or services is referred to as an "importer" and is based in the country of import .On the other hand, the overseas-based seller is referred to as an "exporter."
   - A country seeks for its welfare by importing a broad range of necessary and higher-quality goods and services, that it cannot produce domestically, or requires higher costs in case of domestic production.
   - According to Ricardo, a country imports those goods in which it has a comparative disadvantage.

4. **Exports:**
   - Exporting involves sale of goods and services to a buyer located in a foreign country. In other words, goods are shipped from the domestic country to a foreign country. The goods are produced domestically, and exported overseas.
   - The seller of these goods and services is referred to as an "exporter" who is based in the country of export. On the other hand, overseas based buyer is referred to as an "importer".

5. **Entrepot:**
   - In an entrepot trade, the goods imported into a country are re-exported. This package does not undergo any repackaging or additional processing.
   - Origins - *entry port trade* (avoids the payment of any import or export duties when the package is sent out from that port). Entrepot is mainly used to refer to duty-free ports having high volume of re-export trade
   - In an Entrepot trade, the goods are imported in a country with the sole purpose of getting them to some another country. A different country. Such a trader conducting Entrepot trade thus, becomes both the importer and the exporter for these goods.
   - For example, if an Indian company were to import foodgrains from Bangladesh and export it immediately to USA, this would be called entrêpot trade for India.

6. **Multinational Corporations (MNC's)**
   - MNCs are business entities with investments and operations in more than one country.

- MNCs are viewed in sync with globalization as they play a important role in the free movement of capital, labour, goods, and services across borders.
- Some MNC's have become so large that their revenues are larger than the GDPs of some countries.
- Multinational corporations seek for locations with a business friendly climate and potential market for its products are friendliest and the potential for returns is highest—typically, in countries with low taxes.
- MNC's contribute to economic growth and innovation for the host country.

7. **International Business Law:**
   - International business law expands basic concepts of business law to the international arena.
   - Internal business law differs by jurisdiction and emphasizes on the law as it relates to finance and international transactions.
   - Before entering a foreign market, the business entity should learn about those jurisdictions, analyze the specific laws for each, and then select the best possible jurisdiction for a given transaction.

8. **Trade Agreements:**
   - Trade agreements determine specific aspect of trade or commerce, between two or more countries.
   - Analysing different trade agreements amongst countries can help a business concern in selecting a jurisdiction for commercial transactions. Tariffs and other mechanisms need to be negotiated according to jurisdiction.

9. **Intellectual Property Rights (IPR):**
   - The intellectual property consists of patents, copyrights, and trademark.
   - Such rights of one company can be licensed to another company in different countries, with each license individually negotiated.
   - This ensures that the rights of the intellectual property holder are maintained by each company in their commercial transactions.
   - Additionally, laws regarding negotiation of intellectual property may differ from one jurisdiction to the other.

10. **International Finance:**
    - International finance deals with various components of finance, such as a balance of payments (BOP), foreign exchange market, and financial markets
    - Understanding elements of international finance can help to determine influence of state economic actors in international markets, as well as other nations and their policymaking.
    - Depending upon the openness of the economy to the global capital flow, elements of international finance are affected. A global market's performance can affect monetary and fiscal policies of nations, which in turn, can affect other countries and markets.

2.4   PESTEL MODEL (POLITICAL, ECONOMIC, SOCIAL, TECHNOLOGICAL, ENVIRONMENTAL AND LEGAL)

2.4.1 PESTEL Model

PESTEL analysis is a tool used when starting a new business or entering a foreign market. PESTEL is an important tool used for market and environmental analysis and to assist strategic decision-making. It is true that industry factors have a significant impact on the performance of a business concern. However, a number of external factors also play an important role in determining the degree of success of a business. These are actually macro-environmental factors that are found to have a profound impact on an organisation's performance. These very factors are covered in PESTEL analysis. They make up the acronym PESTEL, as

    P - Political factors

    E - Economic factors

    S - Social factors

    T - Technological factors

    E - Environmental factors

    L - Legal factors

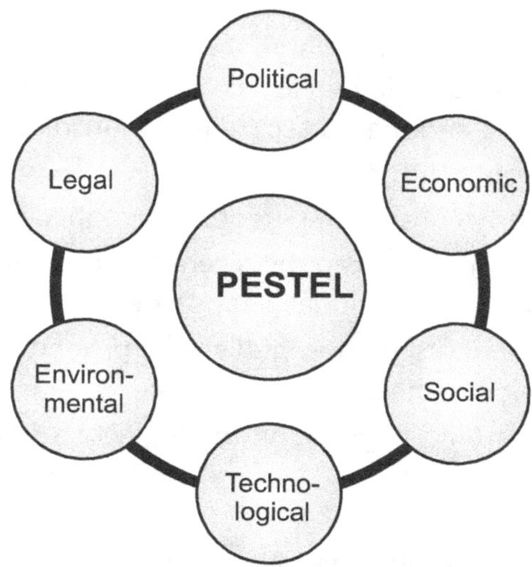

Fig. 2.2: PESTEL factors

Some experts have tried to expand the PESTEL framework with inclusion of factors such as Demographics, Intercultural, Ethical and Ecological. PESTEL tool is used by several organizations as it is effective in projecting the growth of a company in terms of its revenue, profitability and overall success. PESTEL helps an rganization to identify threats and weaknesses which is used in a SWOT analysis. Through the PESTEL analysis, a business can conduct a situational analysis, in order to develop its strategy and/or tactical plans.

Business entities that successfully monitor and respond to changes in the macro-environment are able to create a competitive advantage for themselves, and stand out from the competition.

Other forms of PESTEL

Some experts have tried to expand the PESTEL framework with inclusion of a few additional macro-environmental factors. The developed variants include:

- PEST (Political, Economic, Social, Technological).
- PESTLIED (Political, Economic, Social, Technological, Legal, International, Environmental and Demographic).
- STEEPLE (Social, Technological, Economic, Environmental, Political, Legal and Ethical).
- STEEPLED (Social, Technological, Economic, Environmental, Political, Legal, Education and Demographic).

We shall try to understand the PESTEL factors:

1. Political Factors: Government intervenes in the economy or a certain industry to a certain degree. Political factors refer to the influences that a government has on a business, or on a specific industry or a sector.

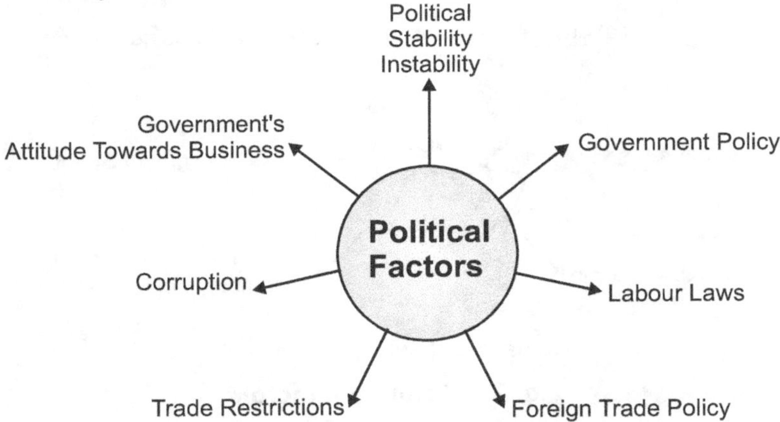

Fig. 2.3: Political factors

Political environment includes legislature, executive and judiciary Furthermore, the government may have a profound impact on a nation's education system, infrastructure and health regulations. The political environment of a country is influenced by the political organizations, philosophy of political parties, ideology of government or party in power, nature and extent of bureaucracy influence of primary groups etc., which in turn can influence the conduct of business.

Political factors include:

- Government policy.
- Political stability or instability.
- Corruption.

- Foreign trade policy.
- Environmental law.
- Tax policy.
- Labour laws.
- Trade restrictions.
- Employment laws.
- Safety regulations.
- Influential political leaders in the country and their thoughts regarding businesses.
- Governing bodies.

2. Economic Factors: Economic factors determine the performance of a nation's economy. Economic factors have significantly influence the way in which a business functions, as well as its profitability. This is because economic factors affect the purchasing power of consumers and can possibly change demand and/or supply models in the economy. These very economic factors will thus determine the pricing strategies of a business concern.

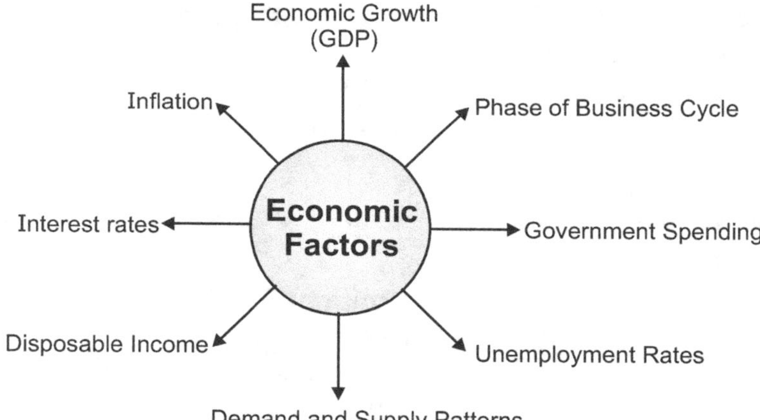

Fig. 2.4: Economic factors

Economic factors are further categorized into macro-economical and micro-economical factors. Macro-economical factors deal with the overall economy (at an aggregate level), which looks for parameters such as interest rates, inflation, national income, monetary policy, taxation policy, fiscal policy particularly government expenditure etc.

Micro-economic factors deal with individuals or households, and try to analyse demand and supply curves, as well as the way people spend their incomes.

Economic factors include:

- Economic growth (measured by GDP).
- Current Interest rates prevailing in the economy.
- Exchange rates.
- Inflation.

- unemployment rate.

- Disposable income in the hands of consumers.

- Phase of the trade cycle (boom, recession etc.).

3. Social Factors: Also referred to as socio-cultural factors. Social factors represent shared belief and attitudes of the population. Things that are prevailing in a society greatly affects the business. Therefore, it is important to analyse social factors while making important business decisions. Cultural and demographic aspects are an important part in social factors.

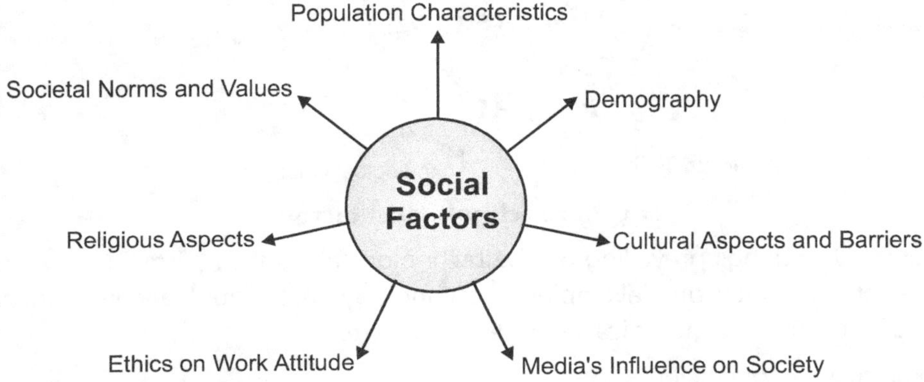

Fig. 2.5: Social factors

Analysis of social factors can help organizations majorly in two aspects:

(i) Marketers when targeting certain customers.

(ii) Human resource (HR) department can get inputs regarding local workforce and its willingness to work under certain conditions.

Social factors include:

- Demographic characteristics of the market.

- Population trends (population growth rate, age distribution etc.).

- Consumer Buying Patterns.

- Income distribution.

- Religious factors.

- Cultural aspects, particularly cultural barriers.

- State and influence of the media on the society.

- Lifestyle trends and attitudes.

- Health consciousness amongst people.

- Career and work attitudes.

4. Technological Factors: Technological factors refer to innovations in technology that may affect the operations of the industry and the market favourably or unfavourably. These factors determine a firm's decision regarding entering into certain industries, or launching certain products ,or certain outsourcing decisions related to production.

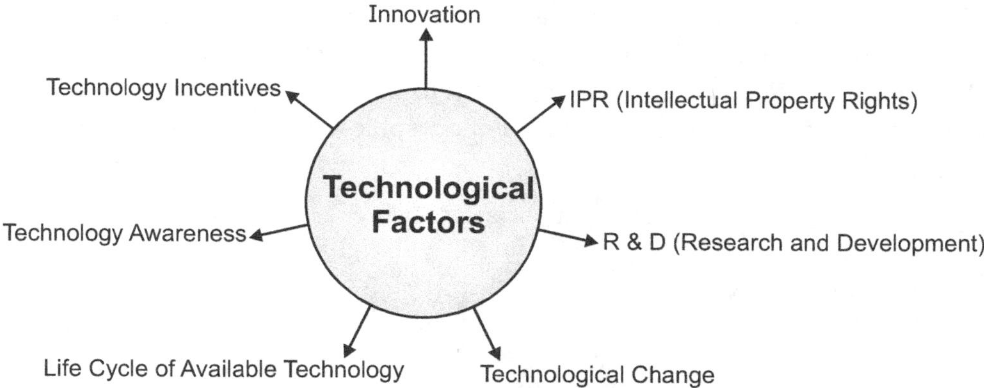

Fig. 2.6: Technological factors

By knowing the things prevailing on the technological front the firm can save itself from spending a lot of money on developing a technology that would become obsolete very soon due to disruptive technological changes elsewhere.

Technological factors include:

- Technology incentives.
- New production technology.
- New innovations.
- Automation.
- Safeguarding of Intellectual Property Rights (Patents, Copyright, Trademark).
- Research and development (R & D) activity.
- Technological change.
- Maturity of technology.
- Obsolescence of technology.
- Technological awareness that a market possesses.
- Innovative ways of distributing goods and services.
- Innovative ways of communicating with target markets.
- Government expenditure on technology.
- Lifecycle of available technology.

5. Environmental Factors: Environmental factors comprise ecological and environmental aspects. Environmental factors have received attention in the past two decades due to the increasing scarcity of raw materials, pollution targets, doing business as an ethical and sustainable company, and carbon footprint targets set by governments.

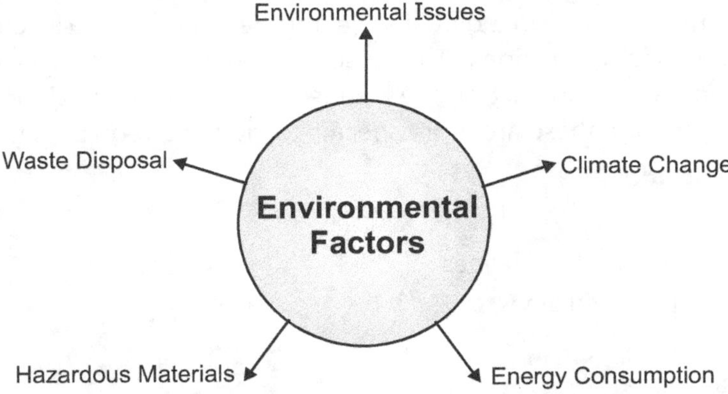

Fig. 2.7: Environmental factors

In fact, the potential impacts of climate change has led to many companies getting more and more involved in corporate social responsibility (CSR) and sustainability aspects. Even consumers are demanding that the products they buy are sourced ethically, and possibly from a sustainable source, and produced without harming the environment .

Environmental factors include:

- Environmental Issues.
- Energy and / or Power consumption.
- Climate change.
- Insurance policies.
- Weather and climate.
- Safe waste disposal.
- Dealing with hazardous material.

6. Legal Factors: Legal factors refer to the laws, rules and regulations made by the government that the business entity has to follow in order to continue their operations. A business needs to know what legal and what is illegal in order to run the business operations and trade successfully and ethically.

Fig. 2.8: Legal factors

When carrying the business on a global scale, this becomes tricky since each country has its own set of rules and regulations. The business has to be attentive to any potential changes in legislation and its impact on the business. Some of the legal factors overlap with the political factors, though these are more specific to laws and regulations.

Legal factors include:

- Business laws.
- Environment laws and guidelines.
- Health and safety guidelines.
- Discrimination laws.
- Antitrust laws.
- Employment laws.
- Consumer protection laws.
- Patent and copyright laws.
- International trade agreements and treaties.
- Regional and local laws.

2.4.2 Performing PESTEL Analysis – The Steps

1. **Deep understanding of PESTEL factors:** Thoroughly understand the PESTEL factors (Political, Economic, Social, Technological, Environmental and Legal), in terms of their different aspects and scope as well as the influences they make on the business.

2. **Collection of relevant data:** Collect as much as possible relevant data about the external environment of the business. This can be done mostly through secondary research, as well as primary research.

3. **Identification of opportunities:** After collecting the relevant information, the next step is to evaluate it and identify any opportunities these changes can bring for the business concern.

   Possible opportunities due to changes:

   - open up new markets for the business entity
   - help the business entity to develop new products
   - help the business entity to make its processes more efficient

4. **Identification of threats:** As the changes can bring opportunities for the business, they can also pose some threats to the business entity, which can undermine the business. Identification of threats can help prevent problems, or decrease their intensity. For example, if a decline in a part of the firm's market is impending, it can open up business in other areas

5. **Taking Action:** After identifying the opportunities and the threats, it's time for organization to act on these. For opportunities, the organization should take advantage of them. At the same time, the organization must take suitable measures to eliminate or manage significant risks.

2.4.3 Importance of PESTEL Analysis

PESTEL Analysis is an important tool, particularly when it comes to making an entry in foreign markets. Its importance is discussed below:

- PESTEL analysis assists management in the decision-making process and urges proactive actions. The business now is in a driver's seat, as it does not merely react to the changes in the environment, but is on a path of converting opportunities into results.

- Economic Analysis helps the organization to develop effective pricing strategies.

- PESTEL is used widely when an organization wants to make an entry into a foreign market.

- PESTEL framework is comprehensive and inclusive and hence, comparatively easy to understand and implement.

- Social factors help marketers understand customers and what drives them and hence in targeting certain customers.

- PESTEL is an important tool used for market and environmental analysis and to assist strategic decision-making.

- Analysis of Legal factors help the organization determine whether there exist any laws or any possibility of potential laws that may highly impact the organization, and thereby provide an opportunity to respond and prepare.

- PESTEL helps in effective long-term strategic planning

2.5   GEOGRAPHICAL INDICATION (GI)

2.5.1 Concept of GI

- According to WIPO **(World Intellectual Property Organization)**, *"A geographical indication (GI) is a sign used on products that have a specific geographical origin and possess qualities or a reputation that are due to that origin".* For example, Basmati Rice.

- According to **TRIPS Agreement of WTO**, *A geographical indication (GI) is defined as "an indication which identifies a good as originating in the territory of a Member, or a regional locality in that territory, where a given quality, reputation or other characteristic of the good is essentially attributable to its geographical origin."*

- Thus, GI is basically attributable to the geographical origin of the product. In order to function as a GI, name or sign must identify a product as originating in a given place, corresponding to a specific geographical location or origin (town, region, or country). In addition, the qualities, characteristics or reputation of the product should be fundamentally due to the place of origin. As a result, a clear link exists between the product and its original place of production.

- Geographical indications are typically used for agricultural products, food products, handicrafts, drinks and industrial products. Usually, a GI consists of the name of the place of origin of the good symbols commonly associated with a place. For example, Darjeeling Tea, Nagpur Oranges.

- GI is a form of intellectual property (IP). GI protection is granted through the TRIPS (Trade Related Intellectual Property Rights) Agreement of WTO. Paris Convention refers to "indications of source" and "appellations of origin" as objects of industrial property.

- India has received several GI, thanks to country's diversity and a testament to the uniqueness of its regions. Moreover, there are products with two geographical indications, one for the name and another for the logo.

- GI tag is valid for a decade, after which it can be renewed for another 10 years. In India, the GI tag is governed by the Geographical Indication of Goods (Registration and Protection) Act which came into force in 1999. Department for promotion of industry and internal trade, Commerce ministry is responsible for registering GIs in India. Darjeeling tea became the first GI tagged product in the country in 2004-05.

- Protection for GI is usually obtained by acquiring a right over the sign that constitutes the indication. Various methods to protect GI include collective or certification marks, and methods focusing on business practices.

- A GI protection (right) enables the right-holder to use the indication to prevent its use by a third party whose product does not conform to the applicable standards. For example, in the jurisdictions in which the Darjeeling GI is protected, producers of Darjeeling tea can exclude use of the term "Darjeeling" for tea not grown in their tea gardens or not produced according to the standards set out in the code of practice for the geographical indication.

- However, a protected GI does not enable the holder to prevent someone from making a product using the same techniques as those set out in the standards for that indication.

    Examples: Scotch whisky (Scotland), Champagne (France).

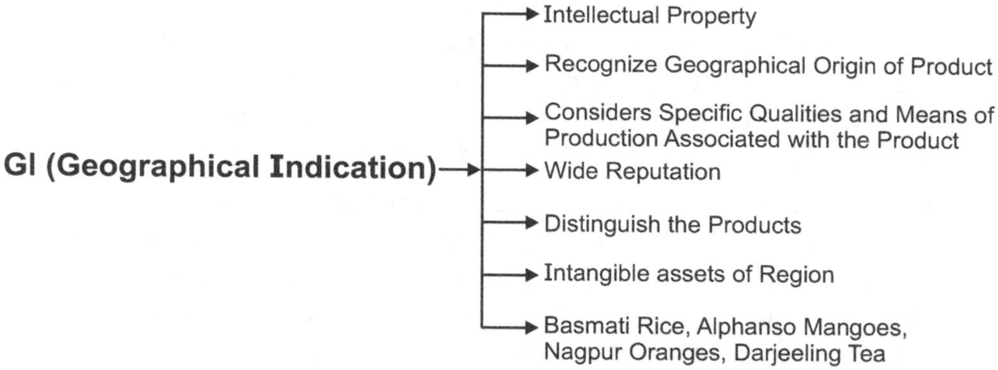

Fig. 2.9: Geographical Indication (GI)

2.5.2 Nature of GI

GI is a form of intellectual property, albeit different from other types of Intellectual property like patents and copyrights. Its nature can be explained as follows:

1. GI is a form of Intellectual Property as per TRIPS agreement of WTO.

2. GI is fundamentally attributable to the geographical place of origin of the product.

3. GI tag recognises the place of origin of a product and the specific qualities or means of production associated with it.

4. GI is basically used for products with a specific geographical location, with a wide reputation.

5. GI tag helps distinguish to distinguish the distinctive nature of products, from look alikes and similar products produced elsewhere.

6. Countries and regions crave for the coveted GI tag.

7. Owing to GI protection, no other producer can misuse the name to market similar products. For example, one cannot sell oranges, branded as 'Nagpur Oranges' unless they are specifically produced in Nagpur.

2.5.3 Importance of GI

When GI protection is obtained, it provides several advantages for the genuine producers of the product of the region. The importance of GI is detailed below:

- GI serve as an intangible assets for the region.
- GI facilitates product differentiation. For example, Alphonso mangoes.
- GI protection prevents unauthorized use of GI by other entities.
- GI serves as a claim to unique fame, presenting several lucrative opportunities.

Similar to intellectual properties rights such as Copyright, Patent and Trademark, Geographical Indication (GI) tag gives rights and protection to the holders of GI.

GI tag offers protection to the producer of genuine products, that command premium pricing in domestic and international markets.

- For customers, GI serves as a mark of authenticity.
- GI indicates creation of added value.
- GI tag helps to get an identity in international markets.

Points to Remember

1. Trade refers to buying and selling of goods and services for money or an equivalent of money.

2. **Categories of Trade:**

    (a) National Trade / International Trade.

    (b) International Trade / Foreign Trade.

3. **Components of National Business Environment:**

    (a) Internal environment.

    (b) External environment.

4. **Components of International Business Environment:**

    (a) International trade

    (b) Countertrade

    (c) Imports

    (d) Exports

    (e) Entrepot.

    (f) MNCs

    (g) International business law

    (h) Trade agreements

    (i) Intellectual property rights

    (j) International finance.

5. **PESTEL Model:** It is an important tool used for market and environment analysis and to assist strategic decision-making.

6. GI is a form intellectual property as per TRIPs agreement of WTO.

Questions for Discussion

1. What is trade? Explain the concept of National trade.

2. What is trade? Explain the concept of International trade.

3. Explain contribution of National trade in the modern world/economy.

4. Explain contribution of International trade in the modern world/economy.

5. What is National business? Explain the components of National business.

6. What is International business? Explain the components of International business.

7. Elucidate the steps for performing PESTEL analysis.

8. Explain the concept of GI (Geographical Indications), along with its nature and importance.

Write short notes on :

1. Export trade.

2. Import trade.

3. Countertrade.

4. International trade.

5. Political factors in PESTEL model.

6. Economic factors in PESTEL model.

7. Social factors in PESTEL model.

8. Technological factors in PESTEL model.

9. Environmental factors in PESTEL model.

10. Legal factors in PESTEL model.

11. Macro-environment of a business.

12. Micro-environment of a business.

13. Multinational Corporations.

14. Importance of PESTEL analysis.

15. GI (Geographical Indications).

16. Entrepot Trade.

Multiple Choice Questions:

1. Trade that refers to buying and selling of goods and services between individuals or corporate of two or more countries.

    (a) Foreign Trade
    (b) National Trade
    (c) Domestic Trade
    (d) Inland Trade

2. GI stands for ......

    (a) Geographical Indications
    (b) General Indicators
    (c) General Indices
    (d) None of these

3. Trade in which the goods imported into a country are re-exported.

    (a) Export
    (b) Import
    (c) Entrepot
    (d) All of these

4. Which of the following is not a factor of external business environment?

    (a) Technological Advancement
    (b) Financial Capabilities
    (c) Legal Environment
    (d) Socio-cultural Environment
    (e) Economic Environment

5. In PESTEL S stands for ......

    (a) Social
    (b) Systematic
    (c) Socialist
    (d) None of these

6. WIPO stands for ......

    (a) World Intellectual Property Organization

    (b) World Integrated Property Organization

    (c) World Intellectual Proposed Organization

    (d) None of these

7. GI is what kind of asset ......

    (a) Current Asset   (b) Fixed Asset

    (c) Tangible Asset   (d) Intangible Asset

Answer to MCQ's

(1) - (a),   (2) - (a),   (3) - (c),   (4) - (b),   (5) - (a),   (6) - (a),   (7) - (d)

Chapter 3

Theories of International Trade

Contents ...

3.1   Introduction
3.2   International Trade Theories
3.3   Trade Barriers
    3.3.1   Introduction to Trade Barriers
    3.3.2   Tariff Barriers (Monetary Based)
    3.3.3   Non-Tariff Barriers
3.4   National tax
- Points to Remember
- Questions for Discussion

Learning Objectives ...

- To develop an understanding about trade theories and its role in determining trade among countries.
- To understand various commercial policies adopted by the nations to facilitate trade between them.
- To study various measures and types of barriers faced by nations and its challenges.

3.1   INTRODUCTION

Trade refers to buying and selling of goods and services for money or an equivalent of money. In other words, transfer or exchange of goods and services takes place in lieu of money.

International trade is that field of economics that determines the pattern of international trade. International trade came into force with regard to differences in opportunity cost. No country is self sufficient in the production of all the commodities at an economic price. The interdependence of nations on one other gave rise to the development of international trade theories. In order to foster international trade there was requirement for certain mechanism for trade to be established. Various economics from various parts of the nations developed various theories that paved a way towards the direction of international trade. Development of trade theories at different point of time are further divided into **classical and modern theories**. This chapter will bring into light various international theories, their direction and mechanism. It will also elaborate the commercial policy or trade barriers that is tariff and non tariff barrier.

International trade occurs due to-

1. Differences in factor endowment.
2. Varity and quality of goods.
3. Gains from specialization.
4. Political reasons.

3.2 INTERNATIONAL TRADE THEORIES

The international trade theories are further divided into classical and modern which is shown as below:

Classical Country Based Theories	Modern Firm Based Theories
Mercantilism Theory	Haberler's Opportunity Cost Theory
Absolute Cost Advantage Theory	Porters National Competitive Advantage Theory.
Comparative Cost Advantage Theory	Krugman's New Trade Theory
Heckscher – Ohlin Theory	Product Life Cycle Theory

Classical Country Based Theories

1. Mercantilism Theory:

Mercantilism is one of the oldest trade theory. This theory **emerged in England** around 1500 to 1800. This theory revolves around the viewpoint to encourage export and discourage import. The value so received will be in the form of precious metals such as gold, silver etc. These precious metals in respect of foreign exchange will increase the wealth and have long lasting effect.

According to this theory the country should concentrate more and more on its export than its import. Limiting the imports will restrict the outflow of wealth in the form of gold and silver

Mercantilism theory rests on **zero sum game**, in other words we can say win lose strategy where one country lose and another country wins.

Mercantilism was more prominent with countries having colonies like Britain use to trade with their colonies like India, Srilanka etc by importing raw materials at a very low cost and exporting finished goods at a very high cost.

2. Absolute Cost Advantage Theory

Propounded By- Adam Smith (Scottish Economist)

Year- 1776

Absolute cost advantage theory is propounded by **Adam Smith a Scottish economist**. He brought into light that the country should concentrate in the production of only those commodities in which they have absolute cost advantage and export them and import those commodities in which they do not have absolute advantage.

This theory is based on win – win strategy.

Assumptions of the theory: Following are the assumptions of the theory:

    (a) Two Countries Two Commodities: The trade will be executed only when the trade will take place between two countries and will involve two commodities. That is the reason it also known as 2×2 Model.

    (b) Free Trade and Full Employment: The theory assumes that there exist free trade i.e. no trade barriers, even there is full employment in the economy.

    (c) Labour as a cost of production: While producing the goods only labour is taken into account as a factor of production.

    (d) No transportation Cost: Transportation cost is omitted by the theory.

    (e) Internal Mobility and External Immobility: According to this theory factor of production that is labour is perfectly mobile within the country and immobile outside the country.

Adam Smith has further divided the absolute cost advantage into two parts:

(1) Natural Advantage,

(2) Acquired Advantage.

(1) Natural Advantage: A country can possess natural advantage through :

    (a) Climatic conditions.

    (b) Access to certain natural resources.

    (c) Availability of certain labour force.

For instance: The climatic condition of Sri Lanka is optimum for the production of tea, rubber and coconuts. Sri Lanka is not accustomed to the production of wheat and dairy products so it imports these products. Thus Sri Lanka should produce more of tea, rubber and coconut as having natural cost advantage in it.

(2) Acquired Advantage:

A country specializes in acquired advantage when they have certain technological and skill development in their countries. They are in contrast to natural advantage.

For instance: Japan by acquiring labour and technology saving mechanism, came up with the acquired advantage. It exported steel products rather than importing them by enhancing their technology.

To understand it better let's take an example-

Table 3.1: Output per day of labour

Country	Japan	India
Tea	10	20
Electronic Products	20	10

From the above table it can be seen that it is a 2×2 model. Japan has an absolute cost advantage in producing electronic products and India has an absolute advantage in producing tea. So it will be beneficial for Japan to produce electronic products and export them to India and import tea from India. India on the other hand has an absolute cost advantage of producing tea so it should produce tea and export it and import electronic products from Japan.

In the example if Japan puts its full effort in the production of electronic products it can produce 20 units by using less labour as compared to India. On the other hand India has absolute cost advantage in producing tea that is 20 units of tea by employing less labour as compared to Japan.

Merits:

(a) **Boost international Trade:** Absolute cost advantage theory promotes international trade. It specialize a country in producing goods and services at a lower cost, which in return reduces the cost of production. Thus promotes international trade.

(b) **Save Cost:** Attaining specialization in the production of certain commodity makes a country obtain absolute cost advantage. This mastery over a product saves cost.

(c) **Base on Win-Win Strategy:** This theory is based on win-win strategy as both the country gets in return something after the execution of the trade.

Limitations:

(a) **No absolute cost advantage:** This theory says that there should be absolute cost advantage in at- least one product. But there are various developing countries which do not have any absolute cost advantage in any commodity. Thus this theory does not apply.

(b) **Factors of production:** This theory assumes only one factor of production that is labour. It ignores other factors of production which is irrelevant.

(c) **Transportation cost:** Applicability of transportation cost is must when it comes to trade. This theory on the contrary specifies that transportation cost is not present which is not true.

(d) **Absolute cost advantage of many products:** This theory fails to explain the mechanism of international trade when it comes to absolute cost advantage in two or more commodities. This theory is only prevalent when 2×2 model exists.

5. **Full employment:** This theory is based on full employment. Full employment is an imaginary assumption and does not exist in real world. Thus acts as one of the limitation.

3. **Comparative Cost Advantage Theory**

   Propounded By- David Ricardo (British Economist)

   Also known as - Ricardian Theory

   Year- 1817

Absolute Cost Advantage theory fails when a country has absolute cost advantage in producing many products. **David Ricardo** through his comparative cost advantage theory resolves the limitation and developed a theory in his book **"Principle of Political Economy and Taxation."**

The Theory states that a nation should concentrate and specialize in the production and export of that product in which it has comparative and relative advantage. It should import those goods in which it has relative and comparative less advantage than other countries. It is based on the principle that a country should engage in the production of those goods and services in which it has lower opportunity cost than other nations.

Assumptions of the theory: Following are the assumptions of the theory:

(a) **Two Countries Two Commodities:** The trade will be executed only when there the trade will take place between two countries and will involve two commodities. That is the reason it also known as 2×2 Model.

(b) **Free Trade and Full Employment:** The theory assumes that there exist free trade i.e. no trade barriers, even there is full employment in the economy.

(c) **Labour as a cost of production:** While producing the goods only labour is taken into account as a factor of production.

(d) **No transportation Cost:** Transportation cost is omitted by the theory.

(e) **Internal Mobility and External Immobility:** According to this theory factor of production that is labour is perfectly mobile within the country and immobile outside the country.

The theory can be understood with the example below:

Table 3.2: Output per day of labour

	Japan	India
Tea	60	55
Electronic Products	6	2

From the above table it can be seen that Japan has the absolute cost advantage in both the products. But Japan has to undergo a comparative analysis and figure out which product's production will be advantageous. If a comparative analysis is done it would be more beneficial for Japan to produce electronic products and export them and import tea from India. For India it will be beneficial to export tea to Japan and import electronic products from Japan.

In the above example it can be seen that Japan has absolute cost advantage in both the goods that is tea 60 units and 6 units of electronic products as compared to India that produces 55 units of tea and 2 units of electronic products. But as per comparative cost advantage theory a country should undertake the comparative analysis. After undertaking the comparative cost advantage theory a country should produce that product in which it has comparative analysis and import that good in which it has relatively less comparative analysis. So Japan has comparative advantage in electronic products so should export them and import tea. On the other hand India has a comparative advantage in tea so should export tea and import electronic products.

Merits of the Theory:

(a) Gave solution when countries had absolute cost advantage in more than one product. Comparative cost advantage brought into light how the country can internationally trade either having or not having any absolute cost advantage.

(b) It provides a solution for underdeveloped countries. This theory paved a way for them which were never discussed before.

(c) This theory gave a new dimension were it stated that rather than looking at absolute cost advantage start focussing on comparative cost advantage which is more realistic.

(d) This theory is also based on win-win approach.

Limitations of the Theory:

(a) Two countries and two commodities: It has also the same limitation as it is also based on 2×2 model as absolute cost advantage theory. The theory is only applicable when the trade is done between 2 nations. It fails to explain the trade mechanism when it comes to more than two countries and commodities.

(b) Factors of Production: This theory assumes only one factor of production that is labour. It ignores other factors of production which is irrelevant.

(c) Transportation Cost: Applicability of transportation cost is must when it comes to trade. This theory on the contrary specifies that transportation cost is not present which is not true.

(d) Full employment: This theory is based on full employment. Full employment is an imaginary assumption and does not exist in real world. Thus acts as one of the limitation.

(e) No mention of services: This theory only focuses on goods and excludes the mention of services from its ambit.

Difference between Absolute Cost Advantage Theory and Comparative Cost Advantage theory:

Basis	Absolute Cost Advantage Theory	Comparative Cost Advantage Theory
1. **Definition:**	Absolute Cost Advantage is an inborn ability of a country to produce a specific good. Goods are produced effectively and efficiently at a lower marginal cost than other country.	Comparative Cost Advantage refers to a situation where a country has a capability of producing the specific good at a lower marginal cost and opportunity cost than the other country.

... (Contd.)

Basis	Absolute Cost Advantage Theory	Comparative Cost Advantage Theory
2. **Basic Concept:**	It is based on lower marginal cost of production of a particular good in comparison of other country	It is based on lower marginal and opportunity cost of production of a particular good in comparison to other country.
3. **Trade Benefits:**	This theory is not mutually beneficial for both the countries involved in trade transaction.	Both the countries are mutually benefited because of comparative advantage of both the countries.
4. **Cost of Production:**	It refers to lowering the production cost of a particular good in comparison of other countries.	It refers to lowering the opportunity cost of production of a particular good in comparison of other countries.
5. **Production of Goods:**	Countries which have absolute cost advantage of producing good produces the good in higher volume with the available resources.	Countries which have comparative cost advantage produces multiple goods in country which deciding the production of a particular good.
6. **Resource Allocation:**	The absolute cost advantage does not effectively decide the resource allocation by a country for cost of production. As it does not deal with opportunity cost of production.	The comparative cost advantage effectively decides the resource allocation by a country for cost of production as it takes into account opportunity cost.
7. **Benefit to Economies:**	It is not mutually beneficial as it deals in the context of absolute advantage.	It is mutually beneficial as it deals in the context of comparative advantage.
8. **Effectiveness for Economy:**	Absolute cost advantage is not that effective for the economy. It focuses on maximizing production without taking into account opportunity cost of production.	Comparative cost advantage is more effective for the economy. It focuses on opportunity cost of production which help them in decisions like- resource allocation, import and export of goods etc.

5.　Heckscher-Ohlin Theory

Propounded by - Heckscher-Ohlin

Also known as - Factor Endowment Theory

Heckscher and Ohlin theory of international trade explains that trade takes between two countries because of differences in cost of factor of production. Trade occurs between different countries as they have different factor endowments.

The theory explains that the countries which are rich in labour should export labour extensive goods and countries which are rich in capital should export capital intensive products.

Factor endowment theory is based on two factors of production that is labour and capital.

Assumptions:

(a) **Two countries, two products and two factors of production:** This theory is based on two countries, two products and two factor of production that is the reason it is called $2 \times 2 \times 2$ model.

(b) **Identical Technologies:** Identical technologies are being used in both the countries. The production method or ways used in both the countries are similar. Only one way is there to produce products at low cost if the factors of production are available at low cost.

(c) **Input and output perfectly competitive:** The market for input and output is perfectly competitive in nature.

Merits:

(a) **Based on general theory of value:** Not like absolute and comparative cost advantage theory which was based on labour value this theory is based on the general theory of value of demand and supply.

(b) **Two factors of production:** This theory unlike absolute and comparative cost advantage theory for the first time stated the existence of two factor of production.

(c) **Production function:** The H-O theory gives prominence to differences in their production functions.

(d) **Efficient trade due to advantage in factor of production:** According to H-O theory trade occurs due to advantage in factor of production. This point was for the first time implemented in the international trade and provided an all together different edge.

Limitations:

(a) **2 × 2 × 2 Model:** This theory is criticised for implementing oversimplified assumptions.

(b) **Unrealistic Assumptions:** Assumptions used in the theory are unrealistic as full employment and perfect competition does not exist in the real world. It is totally an imaginary phenomenon.

(c) **Homogeneous production techniques:** This theory assumes that production techniques are identical in nature. It cannot be true as technology will vary from country to country.

(d) **Static Theory:** Like other classical theories this theory is also static in nature. It elaborates on certain features of the economy at a certain period of time, whereas the economy and the international trade is dynamic in nature.

Difference between Comparative Cost Advantage and Factor Endowment Theory:

Sr. No.	Comparative Cost Advantage Theory	Factor Endowment Theory
1.	Ricardo explained comparative cost advantage theory on the basis of labour theory of value.	Heckscher-Ohlin explained factor endowment theory on the basis of price theory.
2.	It is based on 2 × 2 model i.e. two countries and 2 commodities.	It is based on 2 × 2 × 2 model i.e. two countries, two commodities and two factors of production.
3.	Labour is only one factor of production in comparative cost advantage theory.	Labour and capital are two factors of production in factor endowment theory.
4.	It is based on one market theory as it eliminates space element.	It is based on multi-market theory as it takes into consideration the space element.
5.	It signifies the gains from trade.	It demonstrates the basis of trade.
6.	Comparative Cost Advantage Theory only takes into consideration differences in labour efficiency.	Factor Endowment Theory takes into consideration differences in factor supply.
7.	In Comparative Cost Advantage Theory, international trade is altogether a separate theory of explanation.	In Factor Endowment Theory, international trade is an extension of inter-regional trade.

Modern Firm Based Theories:

5. Haberler's Opportunity Cost Theory

Propounded By - Professor Gottfried Haberler

Year - 1983

The opportunity cost theory is **given by Professor Gottfried Haberler in 1983**. In his theory he states that opportunity cost of anything is the value that has been foregone. Opportunity cost is best explained with production possibility curve. As resources are limited the country has to choose from the alternative which is suffice and has to forego the other one.

For example: In a given amount of resources can produce either 10 units of wheat or 20 units of maize then the opportunity cost of 1 unit of wheat is 2 units of maize.

This theory is the advanced version of comparative cost advantage theory.

Merits:

(a) It emphasised on simplified general equilibrium model of international trade.

(b) Substitution in production was taken into account by the theory.

(c) Trade under this theory is considered under all the three categories such as constant, diminishing and increasing cost. On the contrary comparative cost advantage works on constant cost of production.

(d) It includes various types of factors of production.

Limitations:

(a) This theory is also based on number of imaginary and unrealistic assumptions.

(b) Viner argues that this theory is inferior to classical theories as it fails to explain measures of real cost such as sacrifice, irksomeness etc.

(c) It did not take into account the changes in factor supplies.

(d) It even ignores the preferences for leisure that is income.

6. Porter's National Competitive Advantage

Propounded By - Michael Porter

Also known as - Porter's Diamond Model

Year - 1990

After the intensive research **Michael Porter in 1990 in Havard Business School** published the reason behind the success and failure of a country at international level.

He propounded four components which the companies should adopt to compete and sustain at international level. The four components are as follows-

1. Factor Condition

2. Demand Condition

3. Related and Supporting Industries

4. Firm Strategy, Structure, and Rivalry

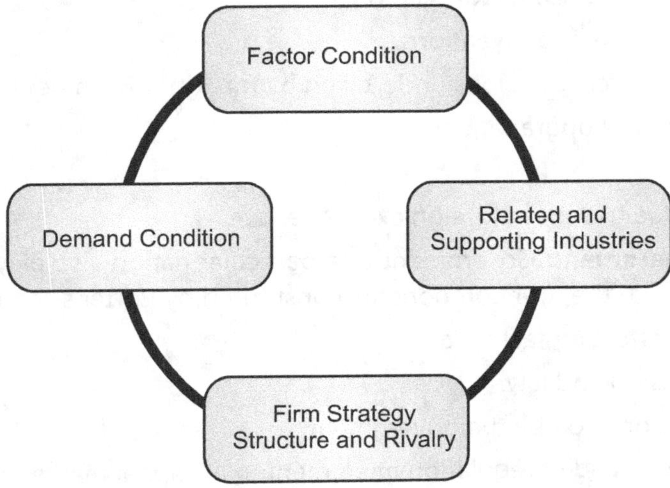

Fig. 3.1: Porter's basic four factor Diamond Model

1. **Factor Condition:** Porter states that condition of factor of production plays a very prominent role when it comes to international trade. As even stated in classical theories a nation having advantage in a certain factor conditions should use them judiciously in order to reap optimum advantage from them. Factor condition can be stated as-

    (a) Natural resources.

    (b) Manpower.

    (c) Capital.

    (d) Internal infrastructure.

    (e) Level of knowledge content.

2. **Demand Condition:** A firm's demand at the domestic market determines its success at international level. According to Porter, a firm that attains a competitive edge at the domestic market can survive the competition at global level too.

3. **Related and Supporting Industries:** A firm working with related and supporting industries attains close proximity and closeness to suppliers, timeliness of product and information flow. This relatedness drives a firm to sustain competitiveness at international level.

4. **Firms Strategy, Structure and Rivalry:** Firm's strategy, structure and rivalry at the domestic market provide a boost to formulation its modus operandi at the global scenario. Thus the atmosphere of a country plays a very important role in the success and failure of a firm.

Apart from the above mentioned components there are 2 other variables namely:

1. **Role of Chance:** Taking proper decision or chance factor provides a great shift and upthrust. These chance factors can be as –

   (a) Innovativeness and Inventions.

   (b) Various political decisions undertaken by foreign government.

   (c) Technological upgradations.

   (d) Wars.

   (e) Impact due to shift in foreign exchange rate.

2. **Role of Government:** Government of a particular nation also plays a very important role to influence the four components constituted by Porter's Model.

   Some of the affecting factors are:

   (a) Tax provision and law.

   (b) Subsidies granted by the government.

   (c) Regulations and deregulation implemented in capital market.

   (d) Product standard set at the domestic level.

Merits:

(a) Porter's Diamond model explains the factors that can drive competitive advantage for one national market or economy over another.

(b) It can be used both to describe the sources of a nation's competitive advantage and path to obtaining such advantage.

(c) The model can also be used by businesses to help guide and shape strategy regarding how to approach investing and operating in different national markets.

Limitations:

The limitations of the theory are as follows:

(a) The theory was developed keeping in mind the 10 developed countries. Thus it is more suitable for developed countries.

(b) The major focus of the theory is at domestic level rather than foreign market.

(c) It is more relevant for service industry argued by many. As its analysis was based on banks and management consultancies.

(d) It does not at all address the role of MNC's.

7. **Krugman's New Trade Theory**

   Propounded By - Paul Krugman

   Year - 1980's

During 1980's the new trade theory was given by **Paul Krugman of Massachusetts Institute of Technology.** This theory states that the organizations that enter the market first or who are the first movers enjoy certain advantages as:

1.   They are able to carve their niche in the international level.

2.   Adopts benefit of economies of scale.

The theory states that due to heavy initial capital investment it becomes extremely difficult for industries to match up with their break even. To compete and challenge the well established players in the market is also extremely difficult. *For example of such industries Aerospace which dominates the airline industry.*

Having dominance in airline industry by few companies their large output which helps them to spread their fixed cost which will decrease the fixed cost per unit. On the other hand if the output is less its fixed cost will be high.

New trade theory is based on monopolistic competition, it explains that brands compete on brand and quality and not only price. All flourishing industries are dominant in capital intensive countries. Developed countries are the one who own these industries thus have very strong competitive advantage.

8.   Vernon's Product Life Cycle Theory

Propounded by - Raymond Vermon

Year - 1966

Raymond Vernon's theory of product life cycle states that during the shift of product life from introduction to decline shifts the location of production. The four stages from which the product goes through as-

1.   Introduction

2.   Growth

3.   Maturity

4.   Decline,

Assumptions of the Theory: The assumptions of the study are as follows:

(a)   The stimulus to produce a new innovative product arises in the domestic market.

(b)   There is no awareness to the innovating firm about the information regarding the condition of foreign market.

(c)   Development of new innovative product initiates in the developed and capital rich economies.

(d)   There is a significant level of difference in the environment of innovating firm.

Stages of Cycle: The product goes through the following stages namely"

(a)   Introductory Stage,

(b)   Growth Stage,

(c)   Maturity Stage,

(d)   Decline Stage.

The detailed explanations of the stages are as follows-

(a) Introductory Stage: When a product is successfully produced it will be introduced in the national outlets. The new innovative products are generally conceptualized in the developed nations. During this stage there are no competitors in the market. The product undergoes tremendous improvement during this stage with the help of feedback. The profit earned during this stage is very low. The customers are unaware about the products.

(b) Growth Stage: As sales of a new firm increases new competitors starts entering the market. The demand of the product starts increasing. The product starts becoming popular in the neighbouring countries. The product slowly moves towards the step of standardization.

(c) Maturity Stage: In the maturity stage the product becomes popular worldwide thus the demand begins to level of. The product during this stage becomes highly standardised. This is the level that the product is at its peak so the producer reduces price to a limit.

Decline Stage: As the product reaches the decline stage its demand in the domestic country starts declining as new technologically advanced products starts entering the market. The firm during this stage shifts the industry from its home country to the developing countries. In return rather than exporting the product they start import the product from the developing country. This situation arises because the demand of the product almost declines in the home country.

Thus from the above it can be seen that during the stages of a product cycle the location of a product shifts from the country where the concept for the same was developed.

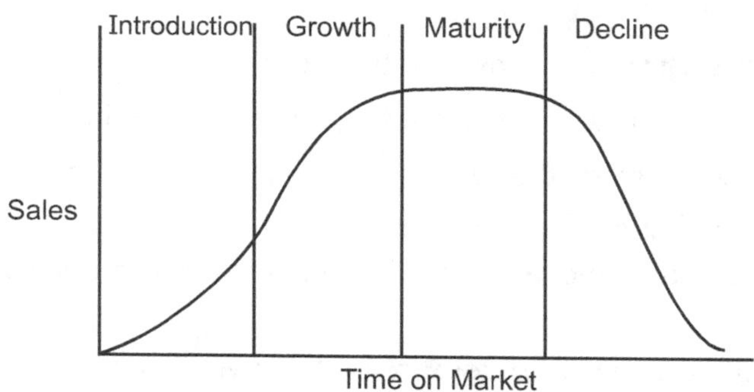

Fig. 3.2

Merits: The merits of the theory are as follows:

(a) This model helps organizations to develop new innovative projects. It helps to understand how competitive playground changes over time.

(b) This theory is an explanatory model how industries migrate across borders over time.

Limitation: The limitations of the theory are as follows:

(a) The assumption that technology can capture in capital equipment and standard operation procedures does not stand true.

(b) This theory neglects emergence of global consumer segment. There are multiple segments available in the foreign market but this theory only includes average income consumers.

Difference between Classical Trade Theory and Modern Trade Theory

Basis	Classical Trade Theory	Modern Trade Theory
1. **Separate trade theory:**	Classical theories state that there is a requirement for separate trade theory for international trade.	Modern theories state that there is no such requirement for separate trade theory for international trade.
2. **Phenomenon:**	Classical economist explained the theory as labour theory of value.	Modern economists explained the theory as general equilibrium of value.
3. **Basis of comparative advantage:**	Comparative advantage due to difference in production efficiency.	Comparative advantage due to difference in factor endowment.
4. **Factor model:**	Classical theory states one factor model.	Modern theory states multiple theory model.
5. **Factor price differences:**	Classical theory never looks into account differences in factor price.	Modern theory looks factor price difference as one of the very important element.
6. **Cause of difference in comparative advantage:**	Classical Theory does not provide cause of difference in comparative advantage.	Modern Theory provides causes of difference in comparative advantage in terms of factor endowment.
7. **Value of market theory:**	Classical Theory is based on single value of market theory.	Modern theory is based on multi value of market theory.
8. **Nature of theory:**	Classical theory is welfare oriented.	Modern theory is based on positive theory approach.

3.3 TRADE BARRIERS

3.3.1 Introduction to Trade Barriers

Trade barriers refer to the government polices and measures which obstructs the flow of goods and services across national borders.

Trade barriers are various types of restrictions imposed on the goods and services crossing the national boundaries. The flow of goods and services during the international trade takes place in the following two forms:

(1) Export,

(2) Import.

(1) **Export:** Export refers to the international trade where goods and services produced in one country are brought by some other country (Foreign Country).

(2) **Import:** Import refers to the international trade where goods and services are brought into a country from another country.

Trade barriers are imposed by a country to adopt **protective measures** for domestic industry and **to safeguard domestic industry** from the competition of developed countries. Trade polices provides a niche or an edge to the domestic industries in order to enhance their competencies by providing various polices as subsidies.

Government announces their trade policies from time to time. These policies are inclusive of both tariff and non tariff barriers. The **trade policies are also known as Commercial Policies** which set rules and regulations which are imposed to restrict imports. Its aim is to boost international trade amongst nations.

Trade barriers are divided into two parts :

1. Tariff Barriers,

2. Non-Tariff Barriers.

3.3.2 Tariff Barriers (Monetary Based)

The term tariff refers to the tax or duty imposed: Tariff barriers are monetary or tax barriers which are levied on internationally trade commodities that cross the national boundaries.

Tariff barriers are those barriers **that increase the rate of import duty**. It does not stop the trade. It only increases **the price of the product**.

1. Non-tariff (Quality and Quantity Specific):

Non-Tariff barriers are those **barriers that restrict or limit the quantity and quality of a product** during international trade. Non tariff barriers **have no influence on the price of a product.** It is a mechanism that restricts the trade from a different perspective other than tariff.

Tariff Barriers from the above it can be understood that tariff barriers are those which affect the price of a product. It does not stop international trade but only makes it more expensive. The various types of tariff barriers are as follows-

Types of tariff barriers:

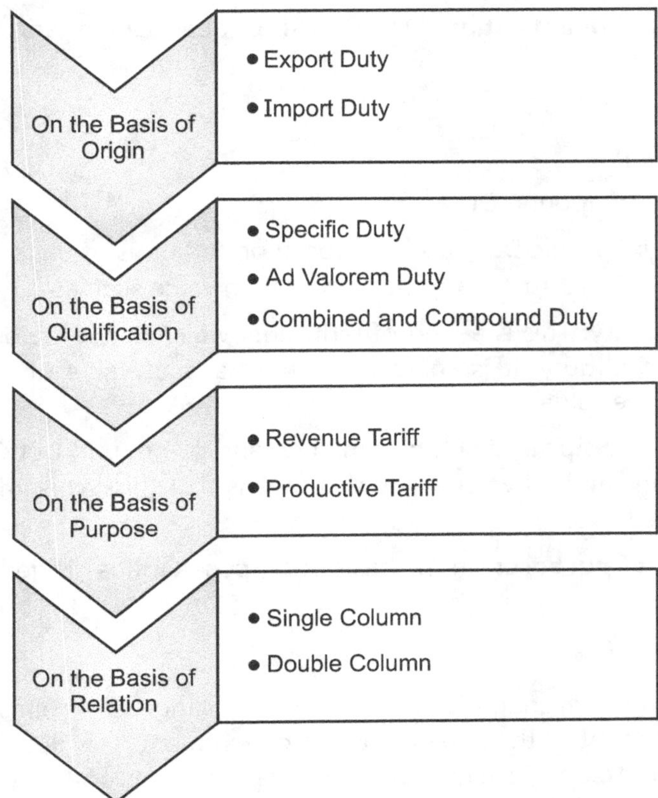

Fig. 3.3: Types of Tariff Barriers

The detailed explanation of various types and categories of tariff barriers are as follows-

Tariff Barriers:

(1) **On the basis of origin:** On the basis of origin the tariff barriers are divided into two part:

(a) Export Duty,

(b) Import Duty.

(a) **Export Duty:** An export duty is a kind of tax levied to the country of use by the country of origin. This duty is imposed in order to conserve the domestic industries. Normally these duties are levied on primary products. In India exports duty is imposed on coffee, tea, oilseeds etc.

(b) Import Duty: Import duties are those which are charged from the country for whom it is designed by the originating country. The main aim behind import duty is to increase revenue and to provide protection to their domestic industries. Countries impose heavy tariff duties to remove the balance of payment deficit by imposing heavy duty.

(2) On the basis of qualification: On the basis of qualification tariff barriers are divided into two parts:

(a) Specific Duty,

(b) Ad valorem Duty,

(c) Combined or Compound Duty.

(a) Specific Duty: Specific Duty tax is imposed on the basis of units. This type of duty is based on physical features of goods rather than value such as ₹ 2 per rice.

(b) Ad valorem Duty: This is a kind of tariff duty which is not imposed on the basis of unit like specific duty. It is charged on the basis of value of an item. It is levied according to the value.

(c) Combined or Compound Duty: Combined and compound Duty is the combination of both specific and ad valorem duty. It means that this tax is imposed on both the unit and value basis.

(3) On the basis of purpose: On the basis of purpose tariff is divided into two parts:

(a) Revenue Duty,

(b) Protective Duty.

(a) Revenue Duty: Revenue duty as the name suggests it aims at collecting the substantial amount of the revenue by the government. This duty does not restrict or obstructs the trade. Revenue duty is imposed on goods pertaining to mass consumption. The rate of duty charged is very low so that maximum revenue can be earned.

(b) Protective Duty: Protective duty is levied to provide protection to domestic industries in order to either eliminate or restrict competition. The rate of duty charged is very high as the government acts in protective mode.

The protective duty is further divided into two types:

(i) Anti-Dumping Duty,

(ii) Counter Vailing Duty.

(i) Anti-Dumping Duty: To understand the term anti-dumping it is important to understand the meaning of dumping

Dumping refers to a practice in which goods are sold in the foreign market below the normal cost or marginal cost to capture the market. This practice has adverse impact on the less developed countries where the cost of production is very high.

Now after understanding dumping it's now very easy to understand anti-dumping it is just opposite of dumping. In Anti-Dumping practice the government of a country adopts strict measures to curb this practice. Thus we can say it is a measure used to nullify the act of dumping.

(ii) Counter Vailing Duty: Counter vailing duty is also similar to anti-dumping duty but is not so severe. These are used to curb or nullify the impact of subsidies or cash assistant provided by the foreign country to its manufacturer. The rate of this duty is proportional to the extent of cash assistant or subsidies granted.

(4) On the basis of trade Relation: On the basis of trade relation the duty is divided into two part:

(a) Single Column Tariff (Similar duty levied),

(b) Double Column Tariff (Two different duties Levied to different nations).

(a) Single Column Tariff: In single column tariff the same rate is made applicable to imports from all the countries. No biasness or favouritism is given to any country. All the countries are treated at par with one another.

(b) Double Column Tariff: In double column tariff two rates are fixed either on one or all the commodities. Lower rate of import duty is imposed on countries with which one has various types of trade agreements. On the contrary the higher tariff rates are levied on countries with which no trading agreements are entered.

3.3.3 Non-Tariff Barriers

Non-tariff barriers are those barriers which restricts trade apart from tariff barriers. These are the barriers which are imposed on the quantity rather than the price of the product. It limits the quantity to be imported or exported without imposing heavy charges.

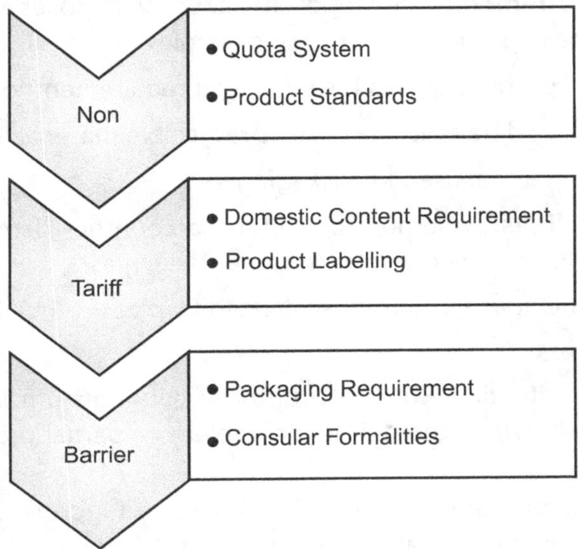

Fig. 3.4

1. **Quota System:** In quota system a country fixes a limit or restricts the import of quantity of a commodity. It does not have any impact on the prices of the commodity as the rate are similar on the restrictions are imposed on the number of products to be imported. So here it can be seen that beyond a certain limit products cannot be imported thus stops trade to a certain level.

2. **Product Standards:** In product standards the country sets the standard of the products that are to be imported in the country. All the products that fall below the ambit of the specified standard are restricted. Thus here the government of a country lays down certain predetermined standards that the importing country has to adhere with in order to get access to the market.

3. **Domestic Content Requirement:** In domestic content requirement the government tries to bailout the organization from an adverse condition. In return the government demands from the organization to purchase goods from domestic country rather than importing from the foreign country. For Example- US bailout package for General Motors where US helped General Motors in time of crisis and in return demanded that they should purchase domestically manufactured products for their organization.

4. **Product Labelling:** The government can even restrict the quantity of a product without hampering its price in case of product labelling. Here the government defines various prerequisites that a country has to follow. If a country fails to follow the requirement the product becomes incapable of entering the country's periphery. For example – the description of the product should be stated in various languages a country which sticks to the entire stated requirement will be welcomed to import their goods in the country.

5. **Packaging Requirement:** The importing country imposes various restrictions on packaging for the exporting country. For example-

   (a) Packaging of product should have minimal requirement for hygiene, safety etc.

   (b) Packaging should be reusable such as recyclable material, biodegradable etc.

   (c) Eco-friendly material used in packaging.

6. **Consular Formalities:** A number of importing countries demand that the shipping documents should include consular documents such as-

   (a) Certificate of Origin   (b) Certificated Invoices   (c) Import Certificates

Other Non-Tariff barriers :

1. **Embargo:** It is a situation where a country or countries officially bans the specified goods for trade between them. It is a complete or partial prohibition of commerce with a country.

2. **Blockade:** Blockage refers to a total ban on all goods and services between countries due to war situation. It is complete restriction on import of all goods and services from a war country.

3. **Health and Safety Standard:** The importing country sets certain standards when it comes to health and safety. The exporting country which abides with all the standards stated will be permissible to exports. These standards are set in order to safeguard the health and safety of the residents.

4. **Sanctions:** Sanctions are imposed on exporting countries to limit the trade activity. It includes stringent administrative action, trade procedures etc that slows down the trade mechanism.

5. **Environmental Regulations:** Certain restrictions pertaining to environment are also imposed on the importing country. They have to produce goods that are environment friendly that has no or negligible hazard towards the environment.

6. **Technical and Administrative Regulations:** Various types of technical regulations are imposed on the exporting countries imposing technical specifications, technical production etc. These types of restriction are basically imposed on pharmaceutical products. Even administrative restrictions are also imposed like documentary procedures to be followed. Thus limits the inflow of goods if the exporting countries does not adhere with pre-determined standards.

Difference between tariff and non-tariff barriers:

Basis	Tariff Barrier	Non Tariff Barrier
1. **Meaning:**	Tariff barriers are those barriers which are monetary specific.	Non tariff barriers are those barriers that are quality and quantity specific.
2. **Hinders Trade:**	Tariff barriers do not stop trade.	Non tariff barriers to a certain extend stop trade.
3. **Restriction on Price:**	Tariff barrier are related with impact on price	Non tariff barriers are not at all related to impact on price.
4. **Restriction on Quantity:**	A tariff barrier does not have any restriction on quantity.	Non tariff barriers have restriction on quantity.
5. **Flexibility:**	Tariff barriers are less flexible.	Non Tariff barriers are more flexible.
6. **Simplicity:**	There is simplicity in the operation. A rate once fixed by legislation requires no individual allocation.	In case of non tariff barriers authorities are there to monitor.
7. **Discrimination:**	There is no discrimination in respect of international trade when it comes to the entry of new comers in the market	There is discrimination between the new comers and the existing players in the market. The policies are different for the both hence discrimination occurs.

3.4 NATIONAL TAX

Those revenue taxes that are levied and collected by the national government via Bureau of Internal Revenue (BIR) are known as National Taxes. On the other hand local taxes are those taxes which are imposed by the local authority.

Types of National Tax: National taxes which are imposed on nationals of a nation specifically pertaining to trade are as follows:

(1) Value Added Tax (VAT).

(2) Goods and Service Tax (GST).

(1) Value Added Tax: Value added tax is a type of a tax is a type of consumption tax. It is imposed on the product whenever value is added to the product at each and every stage of supply chain. It means from the production to the sales.

Value Added Tax is regressive in nature. It is an indirect tax which is levied by the state government it is intra state sales tax. It is charged on the value addition of the product. Germany and France were the first countries to implement VAT. India implemented Value Added Tax on **1st April 2005**.

(2) Goods and Service Tax (GST): Goods and Service Tax is an indirect nature of tax. Goods and Service Tax came into force from **1st July 2017**. It is a **comprehensive, multi-stage and destination based tax.**

(a) Comprehensive: Goods and Service Tax is known as comprehensive as it includes almost all indirect taxes under its ambit.

(b) Multi-stage: Goods and Service Tax is known as multi-stage tax because it is imposed at each and every stage of production process.

(c) Destination Based: Goods and Service Tax is known as destination based tax as it is collected from the point from consumption and not from the point of origin.

There are 5 different slabs for the collection of Goods and Service Tax- 0%, 5%, 12%, 18%, 28%. Petroleum products, alcoholic drinks and electricity falls outside the ambit or arena of Goods and Service Tax. France was the first country to impose GST in 1954.

Goods and Service Tax is implemented to remove the cascading effect and thus provides a common nationwide tax.

Types of Goods and Service Tax:

The types of Goods and Service Tax is divided into 3 types:

1. **State Goods and Service Tax (SGST):** As the name itself singifies it is a tax that is collected by the state government.

2. **Central Goods and Service Tax (CGST):** It is a tax that is collected by the central government.

3. **Integrated Goods and Service Tax (IGST):** It is a tax that is collected by the central government.

Points to Remember

1. International Trade Theories are broadly classified into :
   (a) Classical country based theories, and
   (b) Modern firm based theories.
2. **Classical Country Based Theories:**
   (a) Mercantilism theory,
   (b) Absolute cost advantage theory,
   (c) Comparative cost advantage theory,
   (d) H. O. theory.
3. **Modern Firm Based Theories:**
   (a) Haberle's Opportunity Cost Theory.
   (b) Porter's National Competitive Advantage Theory.
   (c) Krugman's New Trade Theory.
   (d) Product Life Cycle Theory.
4. Trade barriers refer to the government policies and measures which obstruct the flow of goods and services across national borders.
5. Tariff barriers are those barriers that increases the price of import commodities.
6. Non-tariff barriers are those barriers that restricts or limit the quantity or quality of a product during international trade.

Questions for Discussion

1. What do you mean by absolute cost advantage theory? State the various limitations associated to the theory.
2. Write a detailed note on Product Life Cycle Theory.
3. What is theory of National Competitive Advantage? State its components.
4. Explain factor Endowment theory of international trade.
5. Elaborate the term trade barriers.
6. Explain various tariff and non tariff barriers
7. Distinguish between tariff and non tariff barriers.
8. State the comparison between tariff and non tariff barriers.
9. Distinguish between Absolute cost advantage and Comparative cost advantage theory.
10. Elaborate international trade theories in detail.

Write short notes on:

1. Mercantilism Theory.
2. Criticism of Absolute Cost Advantage Theory.
3. Components of National Competitive THEORY.
4. Embargo.

5. Tariff Barriers.

6. Non Tariff Barriers.

7. Dumping.

8. Single Column Tariff.

9. National Tax.

Multiple Choice Questions:

1. Absolute Cost Advantage theory is propounded by ......
    (a) David Ricardo
    (b) Adam Smith
    (c) Heckscher-Ohlin
    (d) Michael Porter

2. Non-Tariff Barriers restricts trade in respect of ......
    (a) Quantity
    (b) Price
    (a) Both (a) and (b)
    (d) None of these

3. Blockade is a situation where international trade is restricted due to ......
    (a) Terrorism
    (b) War
    (c) Peace
    (d) Trade dispute

4. A Tariff ......
    (a) Increases the volume of trade
    (b) Reduces the volume of trade
    (c) Has no effect on volume of trade
    (d) (a) and (c) both

5. Dumping refers to ......
    (a) Buying goods at low prices abroad and selling at higher prices locally.
    (b) Expensive goods selling for low prices.
    (c) Reducing tariffs.
    (d) Sale of goods abroad at low a price, below their cost and price in home market.

6. Factor proportions theory is also known as the ......
    (a) Comparative advantage Theory
    (b) Laissez faire Theory
    (c) Heckscher-Ohlin Theory
    (d) Product Life Cycle Theory

7. Goods and Service Tax came into effect on ......
    (a) 1st July 2017
    (b) 1st June 2017
    (c) 15th July 2017
    (d) 1st September 2017

Answer to MCQ's

(1) - (b), (2) - (a), (3) - (b), (4) - (b), (5) - (d), (6) - (c), (7) - (a)

Chapter **4**...

International Institutions

Contents ...

4.1   Introduction

4.2   World Bank Group

   4.2.1   Introduction

   4.2.2   Organization Structure

   4.2.3   Subsidiaries of World Bank

   4.2.4   Importance of World Bank

   4.2.5   Issues and Challenges

4.3   International Monetary Fund (IMF)

   4.3.1   Introduction

   4.3.2   Purpose of IMF

   4.3.3   Functions and Importance

   4.3.4   SDRs (Special Drawing Rights)

   4.3.5   Governance and Organization

   4.3.6   Issues of IMF

   4.3.7   India's Tryst with IMF

4.4   Asian Development Bank (ADB)

   4.4.1   Introduction

   4.4.2   Operation of ADB

   4.4.3   Organization of ADB

   4.4.4   Importance and Functions of ADB

4.4   WTO (World Trade Organization)

   4.4.1   Introduction

   4.4.2   Purpose of WTO

   4.4.3   Structure of WTO

   4.4.4   Major WTO Agreements/Treaties

   4.4.5   Functions of WTO

   4.4.6   Importance of WTO

   4.4.7   Issues and Challenges of WTO

4.5   UNCTAD (United Nations Conference on Trade and Development

   4.5.1   Introduction

   4.5.2   Objectives and Purpose

   4.5.3   Functions and Importance

4.6   Trading Blocs

    4.6.1   Concept

    4.6.2   Types of Trading Blocs

    4.6.3   Advantages of Trading Blocs

    4.6.4   Disadvantages of Trading Blocs

4.7   South Asian Association for Regional Cooperation (SAARC)

    4.7.1   Idea of SAARC

    4.7.2   Objectives and Purpose

    4.7.3   Importance of SAARC

    4.7.4   Issues and Challenges

4.8   ASEAN (Association of South East Asian Nations

    4.8.1   Idea of ASEAN

    4.8.2   Aim and Purpose

    4.8.3   Importance

    4.8.4   Issues and Challenges

4.9   BRICS (Brazil, Russia, India, CHina and South Africa

    4.9.1   Idea of BRICS

    4.9.2   Goals and Purpose of BRICS

    4.9.3   Importance of BRICS

    4.9.4   Issues and Challenges

4.10   European Union (EU)

    4.10.1 The idea of EU

    4.10.2 Purpose and Objectives of EU

    4.10.3 Importance of EU

    4.10.4 Issues and Challenges

    •   Points to Remember

    •   Questions for Discussion

Learning Objectives ...

➢ To learn about various International organizations in terms of their role and working, formation, purpose and importance; viz. WTO, UNCTAD, IMF, World Bank and ADB

➢ To understand the Concept and idea of Trading blocs

➢ To study the following trading blocs - SAARC, European Union, BRICS and ASEAN

4.1   INTRODUCTION

Trade refers to buying and selling of goods and services for money or an equivalent of money. In other words, transfer or exchange of goods and services takes place in lieu of money.

In the global arena, there exist a number of international organizations. They have been basically formed to help economically deprived countries, restore stability and peace in the world and foster international trade. These international organizations were established by various governments in the world which work together so as to maintain peace and stability. Organizations have even been formed to specifically provide capital and suggest systematic utilisation of these resources and even suggest ways for repayment of debt particularly to those countries that lack adequate resources for their economic development.

The majority of these institutions were established towards the end of world war II , as a part of an overall zeal of mutuality and unity. These organisations obtain funds for their lending activities from two elementary sources, the first being the contribution that each country does when it becomes a member of that institution, and the second source of funds is through borrowing. Today the world's largest international financial institution is the European investment bank whose balance sheet is euro 512 billion in the year 2013, whereas the two institutions of World bank, International bank for reconstruction and development and International development association have an asset of dollars 358 billion and dollars 183 billion respectively as of 2014.

The important International organizations include:

1.   World Bank Group.

2.   International Monetary funds (IMF).

3.   Bank for International Settlements (BIS).

4.   Asian Development Bank (ADB).

5.   UNCTAD.

4.2   WORLD BANK GROUP

4.2.1 Introduction

The World Bank Group is one of the world's largest sources of funding and knowledge for developing countries. The World Bank group comprises a team of five international organizations that provides leveraged loans to developing countries. The World Bank group is a publicly owned financial intermediary that functions like a bank.

1.   About World Bank:

President   : *David Malpass*

Members   : *189 countries IBRD*

              173 countries IDA

Headquarters : *Washington D.C., USA*

Founded in   : *1944*

Mission: The bank's mission is to achieve the twin goals,

(i)   Ending extreme poverty in the world, by reducing the share of the global population that lives in extreme poverty to 3 percent by 2030.

(ii) Building shared prosperity, by increasing the incomes of the poorest 40 percent of people in every country.

4.2.2 Organization Structure

World Bank's structure is organised on a three-tier basis:

(i) Board of Governors

(ii) Executive Directors and

(iii) President

- The World Bank is like a cooperative, made up of 189 **member countries**. These member countries, also called as shareholders, are represented by a **Board of Governors**, who are the ultimate policy-makers at the World Bank. Generally, the governors are member countries' ministers of finance or ministers of development. They meet at the Annual Meetings of the Boards of Governors of the World Bank Group and the International Monetary Fund.

- The governors delegate specific duties to **25 Executive Directors**, who work on-site at the Bank. The five largest shareholders appoint an executive director, while other member countries are represented by elected executive directors.

- The World Bank Group **President** chairs meetings of the Boards of Directors and is responsible for overall management of the Bank. The President is selected by the Board of Executive Directors for a five-year, renewable term.

The Executive Directors make up the Boards of Directors of the World Bank. They normally meet atleast twice a week to oversee the Bank's business, including approval of loans and guarantees, new policies, the administrative budget, country assistance strategies and borrowing and financial decisions.

The World Bank operates day-to-day under the leadership and direction of the president, management and senior staff, and the vice presidents in charge of Global Practices, Cross-Cutting Solutions Areas, regions, and functions.

4.2.3 Subsidiaries of World Bank

World Bank has offices in over 130 locations, and has 5 institutes (arms) working for sustainable solutions to reduce poverty and build shared prosperity in developing countries.

The five arms of World Bank are:

1. IBRD

2. IDA

3. IFC

4. MIGA

5. ICSID

Each of these has a specific mission within a common objective.

1. International Bank for Reconstruction and Development (IBRD):

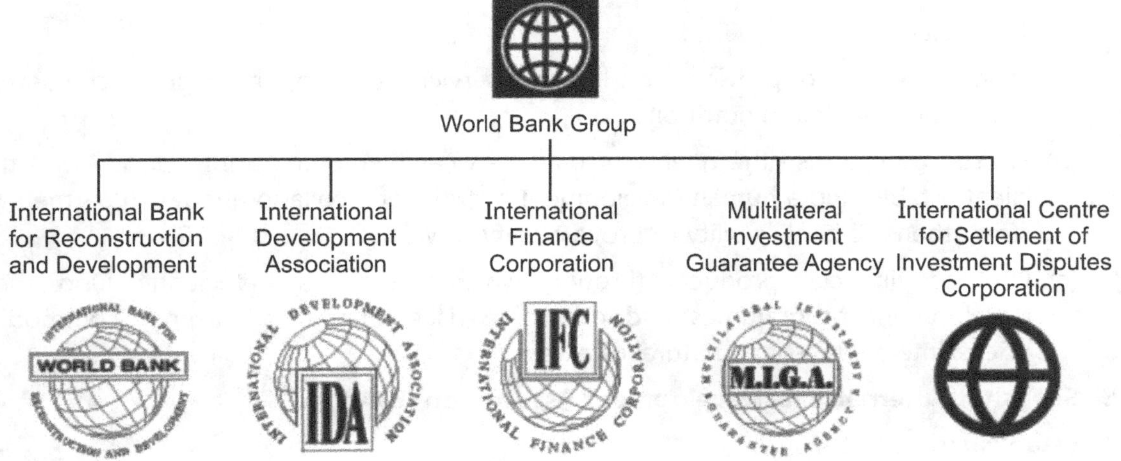

Fig. 4.1

The International Bank for Reconstruction and Development gives loans to governments of middle-income and creditworthy low-income countries. The IBRD is the first in the five institutions that composes the World bank group. It was established with an objective of financing the war ravaged European nations. The IBRD and its supplementary lending arm the IDA are collectively known as the World bank.

The world bank obtains its funds from the capital subscribed by its members, issuing bonds in world capital market, retained earnings and repayment of previously made loans. The articles of agreement of IBRD makes it to promote private foreign investment by means of assurance or participation in loans and other investment made by private investors.

During the early 1980's the bank began to move towards policy based loans which is unlike standard project loans being acquitted in as small as one year rather than the customary five to eight years. They are aimed not at building highway or any infrastructure development but at reaching structural reforms such as an end to restrictions on import or the establishment of market prices for agricultural products. These are of two types, structural adjustment loans for economic policy changes like covering a balance of payment shortfall caused by a structural economic shock, or sector adjustment loans for a specific economic category like agriculture. Sector adjustment loans address to a specific part of the economy. Structural adjustment loans aim to support economic policy changes

Role of IBRD:

IBRD being the largest development bank in the world and part of the World Bank Group, IBRD has two vital roles to play to end extreme poverty and share prosperity, it achieves these goals by providing loans guarantee, risk management products, co-ordinating responses to regional and global challenges and also provide expertise on development related disciplines.

Human development plays a crucial role in the banks overall strategy for reducing poverty.

The bank focuses on:

(a) Lending and also provide non-lending services to support population control, education, health and nutrition.

(b) Efforts to improvise the quality of bank services by working more closely with the client establishing a human development network and collaborating with partners to strengthen the banks ability to prove quality service.

(c) Offering financial products through which clients can efficiently fund their development programmes and overcome risks related to currency commodity prices, interest rates and natural disasters.

2. **Snapshot: International Development Association (IDA):**

   Established   :   *1944*

   Members   :   *186*

   Mission   :   *Broad poverty reduction*

   IDA provides financing on highly concessional terms to governments of the poorest countries. The International Development Association is the largest multilateral source of financing and the main instrument for achieving World Bank Group's two main objective of reducing poverty and boosting mutual prosperity in a sustainable manner in the poorest countries all around the globe. IDA's funding supports countries to increase economic growth reduce poverty and improve standard of living of people. In the fiscal year 2014, 82 countries were eligible to receive assistance from International Development Association.

   The difference between IDA and the rest of the institutions of the WBG is misunderstood they are not separate organizations the IBRD and the IDA are simply labels that the bank attaches to different sort of financing.

   The funding is dine under IBRD label is raised through bond sale in international capital market. The borrowers repay what the bank calls a market rate of interest. The funding under IDA however is much more concessional. These capitals raised not only by borrowing but through subscription from richer member nations gathered in periodic 'replenishment'. IDA funds only the poorest countries. Additional financing comes from IBRD's net income and grants from other financial institutions and borrowers repayment of earlier IDA credit.

3. **Snapshot: International Finance Corporation (IFC):**

   Established   :   *1960*

   Members   :   *169*

   Purpose   :   *Provide concessional terms to governments of the poorest countries.*

   IFC provides loans, equity and advisory services to stimulate private sector investment in developing countries. IFC is focused exclusively on the private sector. It helps developing countries achieve sustainable growth by financing investment, mobilizing capital in international financial markets, and providing advisory services to businesses and governments. Moreover, IFC loan does not require a Government guarantee.

4. **Snapshot: Multilateral Investment Guarantee Agency (MIGA):**

   Established : *1956*

   Members : *182*

   Purpose : *Promote private sector investment in developing countries.*

   MIGA provides political risk, insurance and credit enhancement to investors and lenders to facilitate foreign direct investment in emerging economies.

   It was created in 1988 with an objective to promote foreign direct investment into developing countries to support economic growth, reduce poverty, and improve people's lives. MIGA fulfills this mandate by offering political risk insurance or guarantees to investors and lenders in developing countries.

5. **Snapshot of MIGA: ICSID (International Centre for Settlement of Investment Disputes)**

   Established : *1988*

   Members : *175*

   Mission : *Promote foreign direct investment in developing countries.*

   ICSID provides international facilities for conciliation and arbitration of investment disputes. The International Centre for Settlement of Investment Disputes (ICSID) is an inter-governmental international arbitration institution. It facilitates legal dispute resolution and conciliation between states and private foreign investors. Its aim is to contribute to the promotion of economic development. Since, ICSID is a member of the World Bank Group, it receives funding from it. It is headquartered in Washington, D.C., United States.

   ICSID was established in 1966 as an autonomous, multilateral specialized institution to encourage international flow of investment and mitigate non-commercial risks by a treaty drafted by the International Bank for Reconstruction and Development's executive directors and signed by member countries. ICSID is however, not an international court or tribunal . It merely provides an institutional framework that facilitates conciliation and arbitration. Contracting member states agree to enforce and uphold arbitral awards in accordance with the ICSID Convention.

   ICSID also performs advisory activities and maintains several publications.

A few facts about ICSID:

   Established : *1966*

   Purpose : *International arbitration and Dispute resolution organization*

   Membership : *159 countries*

4.2.4 Importance of World Bank

World Bank's importance can be seen right from its mission statement and objectives, as detailed below:

(i) Accelerating work of economic reconstruction and development in many countries.

(ii) Poverty reduction, by reducing the number of people living in abject poverty, through spur in growth.

(iii) Social and developmental projects contributing to the society at large.

(iv) India has derived immense benefit from the World Bank and has been a major recipient of loans made by IDA on concessional terms.

(v) Several projects funded by World bank has resulted.

(vi) Sharing of its expertise with developing countries, and Publication of its knowledge via reports and its interactive online database.

4.2.5 Issues and Challenges

Though World Bank has been applauded for its developmental role, it has been criticized on the following grounds:

(i) High interest rate for loans, which make it difficult for poor and developing countries to repay in future

(ii) Amount of funds provided is quite less as compared to the financial requirement for various development projects.

(iii) Application of orthodox standards for sanctioning of loans, with regards to capacity of a borrower nation

4.3   INTERNATIONAL MONETARY FUND (IMF)

Fig. 4.2

4.3.1 Introduction

International monetary funds is an international organization of 189 countries working to foster global monetary cooperation, to secure financial stability, ease international trade, promote high employment and achieve sustainable economic growth. IMF makes financial resources available to member countries to meet their balance of payment (BOP) needs.

About IMF:

    Managing director : *Kristalina Georgieva*

    Members   : *29 countries (founding), 189 countries (to date)*

    Headquarters   : *Washington D.C. United States*

    Total quotas   : *US $ 650 billion (as of 3/9/16)*

IMF was established in 1944 at the Bretton Woods Conference, it came into formal existence in 1945 with 29 countries as its member with an aim of reconstructing international payment system. The member countries contribute funds to a pool through a quota system.

The IMF also aims at improving the economies of its member countries not only through funding but by other activities such as statistics keeping and analysis, surveillance of its member economies and self correcting policies.

4.3.2 Purpose of IMF

The primary purpose of IMF is to ensure stability of the international monetary system—the system of exchange rates and international payments that enables countries (and their citizens) to transact with each other.

IMF's mandate includes all macroeconomic and financial sector issues that bear on global stability.

4.3.3 Functions and Importance

1. Stability of International Monetary System: The roles of IMF is to achieve stability in the international monetary system, it does that in three ways:

    (a) Keeping trance of economies of member countries and the world economy.

    (b) Lending to countries with balance of payment situation.

    (c) Providing practical assistance to its members.

2. Economic Surveillance: The IMF monitors economic and financial policies of its 189 member countries, this process takes place at a global level and in individual countries. The IMF highlights potential risk to stability and advises on needed policy adjustments.

3. Financial Assistance (Loans): The core objective and responsibility of the IMF is to provide loans to member countries experiencing actual or potential balance of payment problems. This financial assistance enables countries to build their foreign exchange reserves, maintain their currencies, continue the payment of their necessary imports while undertaking policies issues. IMF does not lend for specific projects like development banks.

4. Technical Assistance: IMF provides technical assistance and training to its member countries to design economic policies and manage their financial affairs effectively by strengthening their human an institutional capacity. IMF maximizes the effect by exploiting synergies between technical assistance and training which it calls capacity development.

5. Capacity Development: IMF works with governments around the world to modernize their economic policies and institutions, and impart training to their people. This supports countries strengthen their economy, improve growth and create jobs.

4.3.4 SDRs (Special Drawing Rights)

The IMF issues an international reserve asset known as Special Drawing Rights (SDRs) that can supplement the official reserves of member countries. Total allocations amount to about SDR 204 billion (some $283 billion). IMF members can voluntarily exchange SDRs for currencies among themselves.

Resources:

The primary source of the IMF's financial resources is its members' quotas, which broadly reflect members' relative position in the world economy. With the recent effectiveness of the 14th General Review of Quotas, total quota resources amount to about SDR 467 billion (about $ 650 billion). In addition, the IMF can borrow temporarily to supplement its quota resources. The New Arrangements to Borrow (NAB), which can provide supplementary resources of up to SDR 182 billion (about $ 253 billion), is the main backstop to quotas. In mid-2012, member countries also pledged to increase the IMF's resources through bilateral borrowing agreements; currently about SDR 280 billion (about $ 387 billion) are effective.

4.3.5 Governance and Organization

The IMF is accountable to its member country governments. At the top of its organizational structure is the Board of Governors, which consists of one Governor and one Alternate Governor from each member country, generally from the central bank or the ministry of finance. The Board of Governors meets once a year at the IMF–World Bank Annual Meetings. Twenty-four of the Governors sit on the International Monetary and Financial Committee (IMFC) and normally meet twice a year. The IMF's day-to-day work is overseen by its 24-member Executive Board, which represents the entire membership; this work is guided by the IMFC and supported by the IMF staff. The Managing Director is the head of the IMF staff and Chairman of the Executive Board and is assisted by four Deputy Managing Directors.

4.3.6 Issues of IMF

Though IMF has provided financial and technical assistance to a number of developing countries and helped them to mange their economic difficulties, IMF has been criticized on a number of grounds

1. **Conditional loans:** IMF loans are conditional on the implementation of certain economic policies. These conditions are imposed on the member country seeking loan from IMF. The conditions can call for implementation of certain economic policies like higher interest rates, reduced government borrowing which implies higher taxes and less of social welfare spending. Moreover, IMF policies also call for structural adjustment via measures such as Liberalization, Privatization, Globalization, Deregulation and reducing bureaucracy.

2. **Supporting Western interests:** Several economists and policy makers have criticized IMF as reflecting the interests and ideology of the Western financial community, and failing to take the best policy to improve the welfare of developing countries

3. **Policies and conditions:** Policies of IMF like privatization have been criticized, stating that it can create private monopolies and lead to exploitation of customers

4. **Little involvement and discussion:** The IMF has been criticised for imposing its policy and conditions, with little or no consultation with the affected countries.

5. **Exchange rate:** IMF Policies related to exchange rate such as forcing member country for Devaluation of its exchange rate, Capital account convertibility have been heavily criticized.

4.3.7 India's Tryst with IMF

By the year 1985 India had started having balance of payment problems and at the end of 1990 it was in a serious economic crisis. The government was close to default. The central bank of the country, i.e. the Reserve Bank of India (RBI) had refused new credit and the country's foreign exchange reserves had been reduced to barely provide the imports for three weeks.

Government of India responded immediately by taking an emergency loan of dollars 2.2 billion from International Monetary Fund by assuring 67 tonnes of India's gold reserves as collateral to recover the balance of payment debt.

4.4   ASIAN DEVELOPMENT BANK (ADB)

4.4.1 Introduction

The Asian Development Bank was conceived in the early 1960s as a financial institution that would be Asian in character and foster economic growth and cooperation in one of the poorest regions in the world.

A resolution passed at the first Ministerial Conference on Asian Economic Cooperation held by the United Nations Economic Commission for Asia and the Far East in 1963 set that vision on the way to becoming reality.

The Philippines capital of Manila was chosen to host the new institution, which opened on 19 December 1966, with 31 members that came together to serve a predominantly agricultural region.

Mission of ADB:

Achieve a prosperous, inclusive, resilient, and sustainable Asia and the Pacific, while sustaining our efforts to eradicate extreme poverty.

ADB had adopted poverty reduction as its overarching goal. With the new century, ADB focused on helping its member countries achieve the Millennium Development Goals.

4.4.2 Operation of ADB

The Asian Development Bank aims for an Asia and Pacific free from poverty. ADB in partnership with member governments, independent specialists and other financial institutions is focused on delivering projects in developing member countries that create economic and development impact.

As a multilateral development finance institution, ADB provides:

- loans

- technical assistance

- grants

ADB's clients are their member governments, who are also ADB's shareholders. In addition, ADB provides direct assistance to private enterprises of developing member countries through equity investments and loans.

ADB maximizes the development impact of its assistance by:

- facilitating policy dialogues,

- providing advisory services, and

- mobilizing financial resources through co-financing operations that tap official, commercial, and export credit sources.

Focus Areas and Results:

ADB operations are designed to support the three complementary agendas of inclusive economic growth, environmentally sustainable growth, and regional integration. ADB employs its limited resources in its areas of comparative strength—the core areas of:

- Infrastructure (water, energy, transport, urban development, information and communications technology).

- Environment.

- Regional cooperation and integration.

- Finance sector development.

- Education.

ADB also operates on a limited scale in other areas, including:

- Health.

- Agriculture and natural resources.

- Public sector management.

4.4.3 Organization of ADB

The Asian Development Bank's (ADB) Board of Governors elects the bank's President. In electing a President, Article 34 of the ADB Charter requires a majority of the total number of Governors, which must represent a majority of the total voting power of ADB's member countries.

More Members:

ADB has 68 shareholding members (member countries) including 49 from the Asia and Pacific region.

Board of Governors:

ADB's highest policy-making body is the Board of Governors, which comprises one representative from each member nation.

Board of Directors:

The Governors elect 12 members to form the Board of Directors, which performs its duties full time at the ADB headquarters. The Directors supervise ADB's financial statements, approve its administrative budget, and review and approve all policy documents and all loan, equity, and technical assistance operations.

Management:

The ADB President chairs the Board of Directors and heads a management team comprising six Vice-Presidents, who supervise the work of ADB's operational, administrative, and knowledge departments.

4.4.4 Importance and Functions of ADB

- ADB has focused much of its assistance on food production and rural development.

- When the world suffered its first oil price shock, ADB increased its support for energy projects, especially those promoting the development of domestic energy sources in member countries.

- Co-financing operations, in which ADB manages the funds of other organizations, provides additional resources for ADB projects and programs.

- Asian Development Fund, established in 1974, provides low-interest loans to ADB's poorest members.

- ADB supports social infrastructure, including projects involving microfinance, the environment, education, urban planning, health issues, and helping women and girls.

- ADB also works with non-government organizations to help disadvantaged groups.

- ADB is the first multilateral organization to have a Board-approved governance policy to ensure that development assistance fully benefits the poor. Policies on involuntary resettlement and indigenous peoples are also put in place.

- ADB provides support at national and regional levels to help countries more effectively respond to avian influenza and the growing threat of HIV/AIDS.

- ADB has responded to unprecedented natural disasters, committing more than $850 million for recovery in areas of India, Indonesia, Maldives, and Sri Lanka hit by the December 2004 Asian tsunami.

Source of Funding for ADB:

ADB raises funds through bond issues on the world's capital markets. It also relies on members' contributions, retained earnings from lending operations, and the repayment of loans. ADB also provides loans and grants from a number of special funds.

Snapshot of ADB:

Motto	:	*Fighting poverty in Asia and the Pacific*
Formation	:	*19 December 1966*
Type	:	*Multilateral Development Bank*
Legal status	:	*Treaty*
Purpose	:	*Social and economic development*
Headquarters	:	*Mandaluyong, Metro Manila, Philippines*
Region served	:	*Asia-Pacific*
Membership	:	*68 countries*
President	:	*Takehiko Nakao*
Main organ	:	*Board of Governors*

4.4　WTO (WORLD TRADE ORGANIZATION)

Fig. 4.3

4.4.1 Introduction

- WTO is the only global international organization dealing with the rules of trade between nations. Its goal is to ensure that trade flows as smoothly, predictably and freely as possible.

- WTO was established on 1st January 1995, and was created as a result of the Uruguay Round negotiations (1986-94). WTO replaced the earlier GATT (General Agreements on Trade and Tariff), which was a legal agreement between many countries to promote international trade by reducing or eliminating trade barriers such as tariffs or quotas.

- The World Trade Organization (WTO) is a global international organization dealing with the rules of trade between nations. These rules are established through consensus among its member states. WTO works for opening up of international trade and makes efforts, so that international trade takes freely, with minimum restrictions.

- At the heart of WTO are the WTO agreements, negotiated and signed by the bulk of the world's trading nations who are members of WTO. These agreements are essentially contracts, binding governments to keep their trade policies within agreed limits. Although negotiated and signed by governments, the goal is to help producers of goods and services, exporters, and importers conduct their business, while allowing governments to meet social and environmental objectives.

- WTO serves as a forum for governments to negotiate trade agreements and settle trade disputes. At the WTO forum, member governments try to sort out the trade problems they face with each other.

4.4.2 Purpose of WTO

- The primary purpose of WTO is to enable smooth and free flow of international trade, as long as there are no undesirable side effects. This partially means removing obstacles to trade.

- It also means ensuring that individuals, companies and governments know the trade rules around the world, the rules are 'transparent' and predictable, resulting in a confidence in these entities that there will be no sudden changes of policy.

Objectives of WTO:

(a) Set up and enforce rules for smooth flow of international trade

(b) Act as a forum for negotiating and monitoring further trade liberalization measures

(c) Resolve trade disputes

(d) Increase the transparency of decision-making processes relating to international trade

(e) Co-operate with other major international economic organizations such as IMF, World Bank etc.

Principles of WTO:

(a) **Non-discrimination :** This principle states that a country should not discriminate between its trading partners. In addition, it should not discriminate between its own and foreign products, services or nationals.

(b) **Open economies and free trade :** To encourage open economies and facilitate international trade. Lowering trade barriers of utmost importance. Trade barriers include customs duties and measures such as import bans or quotas that restrict quantities selectively.

(c) Predictable and transparent : For providing a predictable and transparent trade environment, and for foreign companies, investors and governments to feel confident, trade barriers should not be raised arbitrarily. Such stability and predictability provides encouragement to investment, and creation of jobs. In addition, consumers can thus, fully enjoy the benefits of competition, in the form of increased choice and lower prices.

(d) More competitive international trade : WTO discourages 'unfair' practices, such as export subsidies and dumping products at below cost to gain market share. WTO has provided a set of rules, like charging additional import duties to compensate for damage caused by unfair trade.

(e) More beneficial for less developed countries : WTO provides more time to adjust, greater flexibility and special privileges to the developing nations. Nearly 75 % of WTO members are developing countries and WTO agreements give them transition periods to adjust to the more unfamiliar and, perhaps, difficult WTO provisions.

(f) Protect the Environment : The WTO's agreements permit member countries to take measures to protect the environment, public health, animal health and plant health. The WTO agreements, however, state that, these measures must be applied in the same way, to both national and foreign businesses. This ensures that members do not use environmental protection measures as a means of disguising protectionist policies.

4.4.3 Structure of WTO

WTO belongs to its members. The countries make their decisions through various councils and committees, whose membership consists of all WTO members.

Highest Level: Ministerial Conference:

Topmost is the **Ministerial conference** which has to meet at least once every two years. The Ministerial Conference can take decisions on all matters under any of the multilateral trade agreements.

Second Level: General Council

Day-to-day work in between the ministerial conferences is handled by three bodies:

- The General Council

- The Dispute Settlement Body

- The Trade Policy Review Body

The General Council acts on behalf of the Ministerial Conference on all WTO affairs. It meets as the Dispute Settlement Body for for disputes between members, and as the Trade Policy Review Body to oversee procedures and to analyse members' trade policies.

Third Level: Councils for each broad area of trade, and more

Three more councils, each handling a different broad area of trade, report to the General Council:

- The Council for Trade in Goods (Goods Council)

- The Council for Trade in Services (Services Council)

- The Council for Trade-Related Aspects of Intellectual Property Rights (TRIPS Council)

As their names indicate, the three are responsible for the workings of the WTO agreements dealing with their respective areas of trade. Again they consist of all WTO members.

Six other bodies report to the General Council. The scope of their coverage is smaller, so they are "committees". But they still consist of all WTO members. They cover issues such as trade and development, the environment, regional trading arrangements, and administrative issues.

WTO also has several working groups, like the ones looking at investment and competition policy, transparency in government procurement, and trade facilitation.

Two more subsidiary bodies dealing with the plurilateral agreements (which are not signed by all WTO members) keep the General Council informed of their activities regularly.

4.4.4 Major WTO Agreements/Treaties

1. **Trade Related Intellectual Property Rights (TRIPs):** This international agreement, administered by WTO sets down minimum standards for many forms of intellectual property (IP) regulation as applied to nationals of WTO Members. Intellectual property includes patents, copyrights, trademarks etc.

2. **Trade Related Investment Measures (TRIMS):** For facilitating smooth, hassle-free international investments

3. **General Agreement on Trade in Services (GATS):** A set of multilateral rules covering international trade in services. Several service sectors such as Business, Communication, Construction and Engineering, Distribution, Education, Environment, Financial, Health, Tourism and Travel, Recreation, Cultural, and Sporting, Transport and others are covered in GATS.

4.4.5 Functions of WTO

The broad functionalities of WTO can be outlined as below:

- Administering WTO trade agreements, which cover goods, services and intellectual property.

- Act as a Forum for trade negotiations, which seek individual countries' commitments to lower customs tariffs and other trade barriers, and to open up their economies.

- Handling trade disputes between member countries through a set procedure for settling disputes.

- Monitoring trade policies of member countries
- Technical assistance and training for developing countries
- Cooperation with other international organizations
- Building trade capacity of member countries, especially developing countries.

4.4.6 Importance of WTO

Looking at WTO's purpose, its functions and its major agreements, the importance of WTO can be highlighted as follows:

- Raise the standard of living of people in member countries.
- Facilitate growth and expansion of international trade.
- Reduce the cost of doing international business via elimination/reduction in trade barriers.
- Stimulate economic growth and development.
- Decrease the cost of living for the citizens of member countries.
- Settle trade disputes and thus, reduce trade tensions.
- Increase employment.
- Encourage good governance and protect Intellectual property.
- Provide voice to the weak (countries).
- Support the environment and health.
- Contribute to world peace and stability.
- Facilitate growth and development of member nations.

4.4.7 Issues and Challenges of WTO

WTO has been facing serious challenges in following areas:

- Unilateral measures and counter measures by some members.
- Deadlock in important areas of negotiations.
- Ongoing impasse in the appointment of members of the Appellate Body of WTO's dispute settlement mechanism.
- Trump administration has stated that WTO system has overstepped its bounds in its rules.
- Unable to control strong nations such as China and USA, who have been blocking WTO resolutions, and adopting practices such as currency devaluation, and block appointment of members of the Appellate Body of WTO's dispute settlement mechanism.

Snapshot of WTO:

Headquarters	:	*Geneva, Switzerland*
Purpose of formation	:	*Regulate and facilitate international trade via reducing tariffs and other barriers to trade*
Foundation	:	*1ˢᵗ January, 1995*
Membership	:	*164 member countries*
Head	:	*Roberto Azevêdo (Director-General)*

4.5 UNCTAD (UNITED NATIONS CONFERENCE ON TRADE AND DEVELOPMENT)

4.5.1 Introduction

- UNCTAD, governed by its 194 member States, is the United Nations (UN) body which deals with economic and sustainable development issues. Its focus areas include trade, finance, investment and technology. UNCTAD was created in 1964 with a view that a co-operative effort of international community was required to integrate developing countries successfully into the global arena.

- UNCTAD helps developing countries to participate equitably in the global economy, and access the benefits of globalized economy more fairly and effectively.

- UNCTAD carries out economic research, produces innovative analyses and makes policy recommendations to support government decision-making.

- UNCTAD represents a forum where representatives of all countries can freely engage in dialogue, share experiences and tackle critical issues affecting the global economy. It promotes consensus at the multilateral level.

- UNCTAD turns research findings into practical applications and offers direct technical assistance to help countries build the capacities they need for equitable integration into the global economy and improve the well-being of their citizens.

Mission of UNCTAD:

'Promote development through creativity.'

Values:

Quality, Openness, Innovation, Collaboration, Sustainability.

4.5.2 Objectives and Purpose

- To assist developing countries, especially the least developed countries and countries with economies in transition, to integrate beneficially into the global economy in support of inclusive and sustainable growth and development.

- To implement the global development agenda and assist developing countries in meeting their development goals. These include poverty eradication, improving the well-being of citizens and addressing the opportunities and challenges created by globalization.

- To create platforms for the promotion of the creative economy as a tool for economic diversification and sustainable, equitable and inclusive livelihoods.

4.5.3 Functions and Importance

- UNCTAD promotes international trade between developed and developing countries which have different socio-economic system

- UNCTAD formulates policies on international trade and problems regarding economic development

- UNCTAD reviews and facilitates co-ordination of other UN organizations in the field of international TRADE

- UNCTAD represents as a center for harmonious trade and related issues ,including Government policies of different countries with regards to International trade

Snapshot:

Year of establishment	: *1964*
Members	: *194 member countries*
Headquarters	: *Geneva, Switzerland*
Secretary-General	: *Mukhisa Kituyi*

4.6   TRADING BLOCS

4.6.1 Concept

- Trading blocs refer to formal agreement between two or more regional countries to remove trade barriers between the countries in the agreement. At the same time, trade barriers are kept for other countries.

- Trading blocs lead to trade liberalisation and trade creation between members in the bloc, as they are treated favourably compared to non-members. The idea of a trading bloc is that member countries freely trade with each other, but establish barriers to trade with non-members, which significantly influences the pattern of global trade.

- The member countries in a trading bloc have similar trade policies, with mutual co-operation and allow free flow of goods. Trade blocs have liberal rules for the member countries and separate set of rules for the non-member countries. As a result, they facilitate trade to member countries of the group. However, they block the trade of non-member countries by creating barriers for them.

Major Trading Blocs:

The most prominent trading blocs in world are:

- North American Free Trade Agreement (NAFTA) - USA, Canada and Mexico.
- MERCOSUR: Southern Common Market - Brazil, Argentina, Paraguay, and Uruguay.

- SAARC: South Asian Association for Regional Cooperation.

- Association of Southeast Asian Nations (ASEAN).

- European Union (EU) – A customs union, a single market with a single currency.

- BRICS: Brazil, Russia, India, China, South Africa.

4.6.2 Types of Trading Blocs

A trading block can differ with its purpose and objectives. A trade bloc might manifest itself from simply a free trade agreement, to a economic union.

1. **Free Trade Area:** Two or more countries form a Free Trade Area in which trade barriers (tariffs and quotas) between the member countries are removed, but each country maintains its own tariffs against non-member countries. Example: North American Free Trade Agreement (NAFTA) - USA, Canada & Mexico

2. **Customs Union:** A Customs Union very much similar to a free trade area. The only addition is that member countries maintain a common tariff against non-member countries.

3. **Common Market:** A Common Market is very much similar to a Customs union. Additionally, there is a free flow of factors of productions between the countries, in case of a Common Market. So, no permits are required for a citizen of a member in trade bloc to work in another member country of the bloc. Even finance can move freely between member nations

4. **Economic Union:** Economic Union is very much like a common market. In addition, the member countries in a Economic Union employ the same currency, interest rates and have a common tax system. European Union is an example of economic union.

4.6.3 Advantages of Trading Blocs

A trading bloc results in several opportunities for the member countries. These are highlighted below:

- Trading bloc increases the overall size of markets for firms.

- Trading blocs lead to an increase in foreign direct investment (FDI) as well as the local investments, thereby benefiting the economies of participating nations.

- Trade blocs help in maintaining cordial and peaceful relations between member nations.

- Open trade leads to a faster cross-border technology transfer.

- The larger markets created via trading blocs allow for economies of scale, thereby decreasing the average cost of production.

4.6.4 Disadvantages of Trading Blocs

A trading bloc can result in certain disadvantages, even for member countries, as mentioned below:

1. Trading blocs may lead to a loss of sovereignty for member nations.

2. A trading bloc leads to an increased interdependence amongst member countries in a trading bloc.

3. Trading blocs can result in a disadvantage for non-member countries.

4.7 SOUTH ASIAN ASSOCIATION FOR REGIONAL COOPERATION (SAARC)

SAARC

Fig. 4.4

4.7.1 Idea of SAARC

- SAARC is an intergovernmental organisation and a geo-political union of countries in South Asia. SAARC supports development of economic and regional integration amongst South Asian countries.

- SAARC was established with the signing of the SAARC Charter in Dhaka on 8 December 1985. Decisions at all levels are to be taken on the basis of unanimity; and bilateral and contentious issues are excluded from the deliberations of the Association.

- SAARC is a manifestation of South Asian people's determination towards finding solutions to their common problems in a friendly and cordial manner, alongwith mutual respect and understanding.

- South Asian Free Trade Area (SAFTA) is the free trade arrangement of SAARC

- SAARC calls for regional co-operating on several issues such as Economics, trade, finance, human resource development, tourism, natural disasters, environment, poverty alleviation, energy, transport, science and technology etc.

- SAARC comprises of eight Member States:
    - Afghanistan
    - Bangladesh

- Bhutan
- India
- Maldives
- Nepal
- Pakistan
- Sri Lanka.

4.7.2 Objectives and Purpose

As outlined in the SAARC Charter, the objectives of SAARC are as follows:

(i) To promote the welfare of the people of South Asia and to improve their quality of life.

(ii) To accelerate economic growth, social progress and cultural development in the region and to provide all individuals the opportunity to live in dignity and to realize their full potentials.

(iii) To promote and strengthen collective self-reliance among the countries of South Asia.

(iv) To contribute to mutual trust, understanding and appreciation of one another's problems.

(v) To promote active collaboration and mutual assistance in the economic, social, cultural, technical and scientific fields.

(vi) To strengthen cooperation with other developing countries.

(vii) To strengthen cooperation amongst member nations in international forums on matters of common interests; and to cooperate with international and regional organizations with similar aims and purposes.

4.7.3 Importance of SAARC

- SAARC comprises 3% of the world's area, 21% of the global population and nearly 4 % of the world economy.

- SAARC countries have many things in common such as traditions, dressing style, food, culture, fertile areas, dense areas as well as political facets. As a result, they can synergize their actions to achieve a better whole.

- Almost all SAARC countries face common problems such as poverty, illiteracy, natural disasters, malnutrition, and internal conflicts. Most of the SAARC nations are also industrial and technologically backward, and have low GDP per capita. Common problems can call for common areas of development and progress, having common solutions.

- SAARC reflects the South Asian identity of the countries, historically and contemporarily.

- SAARC looks promising as regards to maintain peace and stability in the region.

4.7.4 Issues and Challenges

SAARC has not delivered as per expectations, and in future, faces a number of challenges on several fronts:

1. The frequency of meetings is low. The meetings are currently held biennially (once in 2 years). For more engagement and dialogue between member nations, it should be held annually.

2. SAFTA, a Free Trade Agreement confined to goods, has not delivered as per the expectations. Services like information technology are excluded from SAFTA.

3. Indo-Pak Relations and the related conflicts have severely hindered the prospects of SAARC.

4.8 | ASEAN (ASSOCIATION OF SOUTH EAST ASIAN NATIONS

Fig. 4.5

4.8.1 Idea of ASEAN

- ASEAN is an intergovernmental organization aimed principally at supporting economic growth and regional stability among its members.

- ASEAN was established on 8 August 1967 in Bangkok, Thailand, with the signing of the ASEAN Declaration (Bangkok Declaration).

- Today, ASEAN has 10 member states:
  - Indonesia
  - Malaysia
  - Philippines
  - Singapore
  - Thailand
  - Brunei
  - Laos
  - Myanmar
  - Cambodia
  - Vietnam.

Motto: The motto of ASEAN is "One Vision, One Identity, One Community".

4.8.2 Aim and Purpose

ASEAN was set up in 1967 during the polarized atmosphere of the Cold War, and the association aimed to promote stability in the region.

As mentioned in the ASEAN Charter, the aims and purposes of ASEAN are:

- To accelerate the economic growth, social progress and cultural development in the region through joint endeavours in the spirit of equality and partnership in order to strengthen the foundation for a prosperous and peaceful community of Southeast Asian Nations;

- To promote regional peace and stability through abiding respect for justice and the rule of law in the relationship among countries of the region and adherence to the principles of the United Nations Charter;

- To promote active collaboration and mutual assistance on matters of common interest in the economic, social, cultural, technical, scientific and administrative fields;

- To provide assistance to each other in the form of training and research facilities in the educational, professional, technical and administrative spheres;

- To collaborate more effectively for the greater utilisation of their agriculture and industries, the expansion of their trade, including the study of the problems of international commodity trade, the improvement of their transportation and communications facilities and the raising of the living standards of their peoples;

- To promote Southeast Asian studies;

- To maintain close and beneficial cooperation with existing international and regional organisations with similar aims and purposes, and explore all avenues for even closer cooperation among themselves.

4.8.3 Importance

- Member states of ASEAN share a focus on jobs and prosperity.
- ASEAN has helped shape institutional development in the Asia Pacific region, mainly since the 1990s.
- ASEAN has led to rise in purchasing power of households in the member nations, driving the region into the next frontier of consumer growth.
- Had ASEAN been a country, it would be the seventh-largest economy in the world.
- ASEAN is a home to nearly 700 million people.
- ASEAN has the third-largest labour force in the world.

4.8.4 Issues and Challenges

1. Accommodation of new members, especially addition of members such as Burma which has substantial internal political problems.

2. Leadership transition can influence ASEAN's internal cohesion.

3. Internal conflicts in several member nations.

Snapshot:

Headquarters : *Jakarta, Indonesia*

Founded on   : *8 August 1967*

Members   : *10*

4.9   BRICS (BRAZIL, RUSSIA, INDIA, CHINA AND SOUTH AFRICA

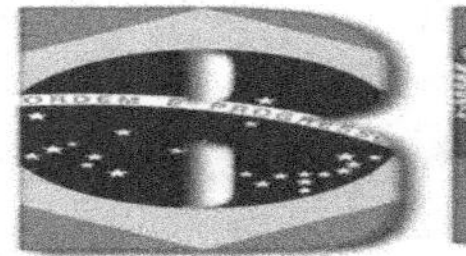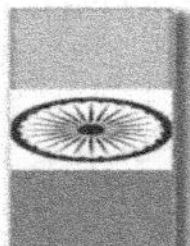

Fig. 4.6

4.9.1 Idea of BRICS

- BRICS is an acronym for Brazil, Russia, India, China and South Africa and is an association of these countries. The BRICS countries have been identified as the fastest growing economies in the world.

- BRICS refers to an informal group of states comprising Brazil, Russia, India, China and South Africa.

- BRICS summits discuss on various issues such as trade, investment, youth, migration, industry, energy, security, peace, environment, fight against infectious diseases ,banking cooperation, agriculture, health, education, development of humanitarian contacts and tourism, poverty eradication etc.

- Seen as a counterweight to G7 (group of developed economies), BRICS represents the world's top emerging economies and claims to work as a link between the developed and developing world.

4.9.2 Goals and Purpose of BRICS

1. To promote dialogue and cooperation amongst BRICS countries in an incremental, proactive, pragmatic, open and transparent way.

2. The dialogue and cooperation of the BRIC countries should be conducive not only to serving common interests of emerging market economies and developing countries, but also to building a harmonious world of lasting peace and common prosperity."

3. Increasing trade co-operation amongst BRICS countries.

4. Increasing regional co-operation.

4.9.3 Importance of BRICS

The importance of BRICS can be understood by the tremendous economic growth and development achieved by these nations over the past 2 decades. Below are the highlights:

1. BRICS accounts for nearly one-fourth of the global GDP, in terms of the purchasing power parity.

2. The total BRICS population is nearly 40 % of the entire global population, and cover more than 25 % of the world's land area.

3. BRICS countries have been showing strong economic growth, amid 2008 crisis and have been the main driving forces of global economic development.

4. As regards to global governance, the BRICS countries play an increasingly important role in participating in and promoting the reform and restructuring of the global economic governance system

5. BRICS countries are influential members of leading international organisations and agencies, including the UN, the G20, the Non-Aligned Movement and the Group of 77. They are also the members of various regional associations.

4.9.4 Issues and Challenges

1. Governance of economic and social issues in and among the BRICS countries is at stake. Example: The Sino-Indian Doklam border confrontation.

2. Economic competition has emerged amongst BRICS nations as their economic structures and development trends are quite similar. Example: Competition for export markets of EU and US. This very completion has also led to conflicts amongst BRICS nations.

3. Severe inflation in Russia, Brazil and South Africa is a concern.

4. Internally, BRICS countries have been facing social problems like strikes and crime.

5. China's political aspirations makes it difficult to reach consensus on several important matters.

Snapshot:

Founded on : June 2006

Founders : India, Brazil, China, Russia

Members : 5

4.10 EUROPEAN UNION (EU)

Fig. 4.7: European Union

4.10.1 The idea of EU

- The European Union is a political and economic union of 28 member states that are located mainly in Europe.

- 19 of these countries use Euro as their official currency.

- The EU was raised out of a desire to form a single European political entity to end the centuries of warfare among European countries that culminated with World War II and decimated much of the continent.

- Free trade among its members was one of the EU's founding principles

- EU is a economic union with member nations having one central bank, i.e. ECB (European Central Bank) which forms monetary policy for the entire EU.

- EU's main economic engine is the single market, which enables most goods, services, money and people to move freely through member countries in Europe.

EU member countries:

1. Austria
2. Italy
3. Belgium
4. Latvia
5. Bulgaria
6. Lithuania
7. Croatia
8. Luxembourg
9. Cyprus
10. Malta
11. Czech Republic
12. Netherlands
13. Denmark
14. Poland
15. Estonia
16. Portugal
17. Finland

18. Romania

19. France

20. Slovakia

21. Germany

22. Slovenia

23. Greece

24. Spain

25. Hungary

26. Sweden

27. Ireland

28. United Kingdom

4.10.2 Purpose and Objectives of EU

EU, raised out of a desire to form a single European political entity to end the centuries of warfare among European countries, has following broad objectives:

- Promote peace and ensure the well-being of its citizens.

- Offer freedom, security and justice without internal borders.

- Sustainable development based on balanced economic growth and price stability, a highly competitive market economy with full employment and social progress, while ensuring environmental protection.

- Combat social exclusion and discrimination.

- Promote scientific and technological progress.

- Enhance economic, social and territorial cohesion and solidarity among EU countries

- Respect its rich cultural and linguistic diversity.

- Establish an economic and monetary union whose currency is the euro.

4.10.3 Importance of EU

- EU has a combined GDP of nearly 18 trillion dollars.

- Formation of EU has led to peaceful and amicable relations between the member countries. In fact, The Nobel Peace Prize 2012 was awarded to European Union (EU) "for over six decades contributed to the advancement of peace and reconciliation, democracy and human rights in Europe".

- European Union is the largest trade block in the world, and the world's biggest exporter of manufactured goods and services, and the biggest import market for over 100 countries.

- With formation of EU, it has become much easier for citizens of European member nations to live, work and travel abroad in Europe . For example, a German citizen can easily choose to live, work or travel to France or any other European nation.

4.10.4 Issues and Challenges

1. Even after a decade after the global financial crisis average annual growth of EU nations remains a sluggish 1.5%.

2. Debt levels of some European nations are rising quite fast.

3. Climate change, ageing population, unemployment, immigration and global security are some of the issues that the EU is wary of.

4. PIIGS (Portugal, Italy, Ireland, Greece, and Spain) were at the verge of default during the European debt crisis. There were a lot of confrontations amongst EU members, regarding providing them a bailout, still keeping them a part of EU, and imposing austerity measures on citizens of PIIGS countries.

5. BREXIT (Separation of UK from EU) can pose some issues to EU. Moreover, with BREXIT, if other EU members follow suit, the very existence of EU will be threatened.

6. The economic crisis of the PIIGS nations reignited debate about the effectiveness of the single currency employed among the Euro zone nations. This very crisis questioned the very notion that the EU can maintain a single currency while attending to the individual needs of each of its member countries.

7. Several critics opine that the continued economic disparities amongst EU member nations could lead to a breakup of the EU.

Snapshot:

Year of formation	:	*1957*
Headquarters	:	*Brussels, Belgium*
Type	:	*Political and economic union*
Number of member countries	:	*28*

Points to Remember

1. World Bank helps to accelerate the work of economic reconstructive and development in many countries.

2. International Monetary Fund (IMF) is an international organization of 189 countries working to foster global monetary co-operation and achieve sustainable economic growth.

3. The Asian Development Bank (ADB) aims for an Asia and Pacific free from poverty.

4. WTO (World Trade Organization) is the only global international organization dealing with the rules of trade between nations.

5. UNCTAD is the United Nations (UN) body which deals with economic and sustainable development issues.

6. Trading blocks refers to formal agreement between two or more regional countries to remove trade barriers between the countries in the agreement.

7. SAARC is an inter-governmental organization and a geo-political union of countries in South Asia.

8. ASEAN is an inter-governmental organization aimed principally at supporting economic growth and regional stability among its members.

9. The European Union (EU) is a political and economic union of 28 member states that are mainly located in Europe.

10. BRICS is an acronym for Brazil, Russia, India, China and South Africa and is an association of these countries.

Questions for Discussion

1. Write a detailed note on World bank group covering its Purpose and Importance.

2. Explain various subsidiaries of World Bank, and their functions.

3. Explain objectives, importance, function and organization of IMF.

4. Explain objectives, importance, function and organization of WTO.

5. Write a detailed note on UNCTAD.

6. Explain the concept of trading blocs in detail.

7. Explain South Asian Association for Regional Cooperation (SAARC) in detail.

8. Explain the trading bloc ASEAN (Association of Southeast Asian Nations) in detail.

9. Explain BRICS (Brazil, Russia, India, China and South Africa) alongwith its role and importance in world order. Also, highlight the issues and challenges of BRICS.

10. Write a detailed note on ADB explaining its role and operation, functions and importance.

11. Write a detailed note on European Union (EU).

Write short notes on :

1. SDR
2. IDA
3. IBRD
4. UNCTAD
5. Principles of WTO

6. TRIPS and TRIMS
7. Challenges of EU
8. Objectives of SAARC
9. ICSID
10. Trading blocs
11. Challenges facing BRICS
12. Types of trading blocs
13. Functions of IMF

Multiple Choice Questions:

1. Headquarter of WTO is in ......
   - (a) Geneva
   - (b) Germany
   - (c) USA
   - (d) Australia

2. Which international institutions are known as Bretton Wood Twins?
   - (a) IMF and WTO
   - (b) IMF and World Bank
   - (c) World Bank and EU
   - (d) ASEAN and WTO

3. SAARC was established in ......
   - (a) 1990
   - (b) 1986
   - (c) 1985
   - (d) 1984

4. In BRICS C stands for ......
   - (a) Cambodia
   - (b) Chile
   - (c) China
   - (d) Cyprus

5. Which among the following is known as the soft loan window of world bank?
   - (a) ICSID
   - (b) IFC
   - (c) IBRD
   - (d) IDA

6. SDR stands for ......
   - (a) Special Drawing Rights
   - (b) Specified Drawing Rights
   - (c) Specific Drawing Regulations
   - (d) Stipulated Drawing Rights

7. World Trade Organization is an outcome of ......
   - (a) Geneva Round
   - (b) Uruguay Round
   - (c) Annecy Round
   - (d) Dillon Round

8. Afghanistan became a member of SAARC in the year ......
   - (a) 2005
   - (b) 2007
   - (c) 2004
   - (d) 2006

Answer to MCQ's

(1) - (a),   (2) - (b),   (3) - (c),   (4) - (c),   (5) - (d),   (6) - (a),   (7) - (b),   (8) - (b)

MODEL QUESTION PAPER

(Based on University Question Paper Pattern)

(CBCS Pattern 2019)

B.B.A. (IB) : Semester – II

Origin and Development of Global Business

[Time : 2 Hours] **[Max. Marks : 50]**

Q. 1: (A) Fill in the blanks by Choosing Correct Alternatives : **[5]**

1. A .... is a closely knit unit.

   (a) Transnational Corporation (b) Domestic Company

   (c) Multi-domestic Company (d) Multinational Corporation

2. .... environment refers to the influence of the system of government and judiciary in a nation on international business.

   (a) Economic (b) Legal

   (c) Political (d) Cultural

3. .... is a customs duty or a tax on products that move across borders.

   (a) Tariff (b) Trading Block

   (c) GST (d) Exports Duty

4. .... is a geo-political and economic organisation of 10 countries of southeast Asia.

   (a) SAARC (b) ASEAN

   (c) ADB (d) UNCTAD

5. .... as the union of the world's five largest developing economies has good potential for growth.

   (a) BRICS (b) SAARC

   (c) IMF (d) ADB

Ans. : (1) – (a), (2) – (c), (3) – (a), (4) – (b), (5) – (a).

Q. 1 (B) : Define the terms : **[5]**

1. Globalization.
2. International Business.
3. International Trade.
4. Geographical Indications.
5. Tariffs.

M.1

Q. 2 : Explain the means of Entry into the International Business.   **[10]**

OR

Q. 2 : Describe the PESTEL Model of International Business.

Q. 3 : Explain the various types of Tariffs.   **[10]**

OR

Q. 3 : What is World Bank ? State its Objectives and functions.

Q. 4 : Write Short Notes : (Attempt Any Four) :   **[20]**

    (1) Stages of Industrialization.

    (2) Geographical Indications.

    (3) Theories of Trade.

    (4) SAARC

    (5) European Union.

    (6) Non-Tariff Measures.